Run, Stroll, Hike

A guide to family-friendly trails in & around Denver

26 Trails Within 40 Minutes from Downtown
plus 12 honorable mentions

by Chris Sekirnjak

Denver, Colorado

Run, Stroll, Hike
A guide to family-friendly trails in & around Denver

Revised first edition (2014)

Published by Chris Sekirnjak

All photos by the author except for routes P1, P2, and P4 by Julie Zavala.
Front cover photo: Alderfer/Three Sisters Park (route F4)
Back cover photo: Roxborough State Park (route L6)

ISBN 978-0-615-84054-3

Printed in the U.S.A. by KIMCO Printing, Denver

For comments or questions, send an email to *runstrollhike@gmail.com*
or visit the book website at *runstrollhike.com*

About the author

Chris Sekirnjak has lived in the Denver area since 2004. For as long as he can remember, he has run through woods, climbed mountains, and pitched tents. He recently became an expert in running with a jogging stroller and decided to offer his acquired proficiency to a larger crowd of active local parents.

He was born in Vienna, Austria, and his parents still live there. He earned a PhD in Neuroscience at UCSD. This is his first publication outside the realm of science. He notes that scientific research is almost as much fun as doing outdoors research for this book (although it usually does not keep him in such good shape).

Chris met his wife Debbie while studying in San Diego. They live near downtown Denver with their kids Kenny and Elena.

Area map and trails overview

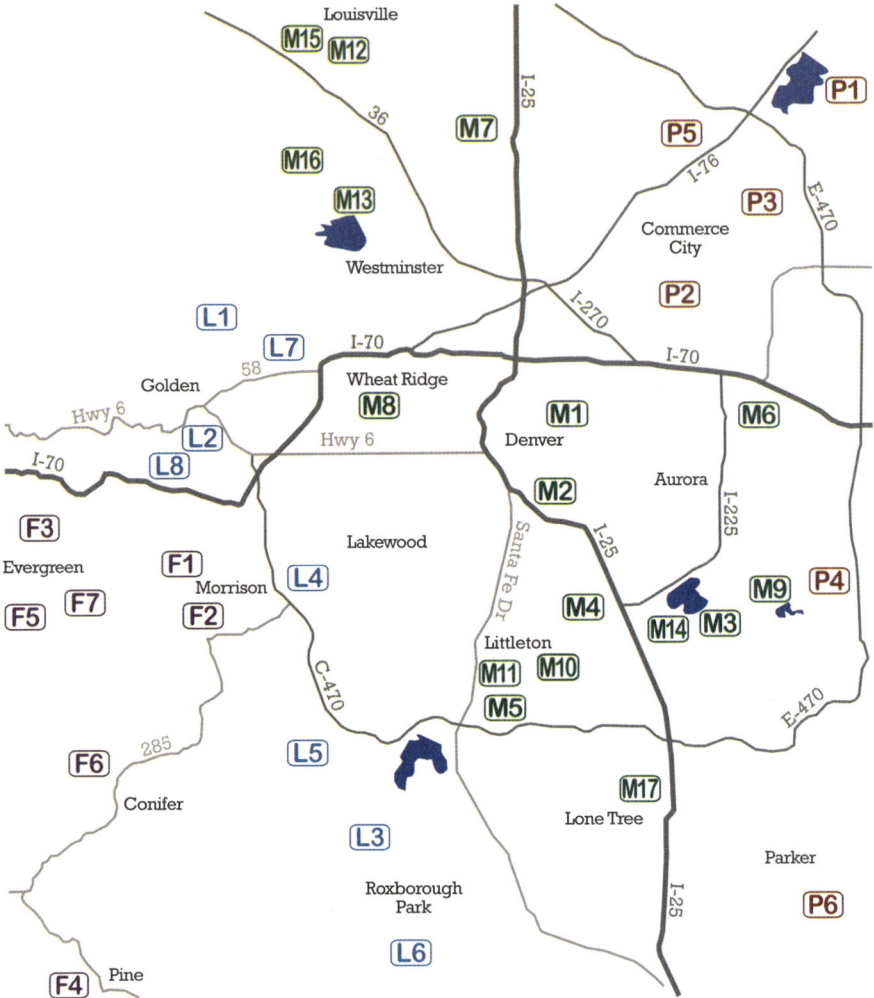

Louisville
M15 M12
P1
36
M7
I-25
P5
M16
I-76
P3
M13
E-470
Commerce
City
Westminster
P2
L1
L7
I-70
I-70
58
Golden
Wheat Ridge
M8
M1
M6
Hwy 6
Hwy 6
Denver
L2
M2
Aurora
I-70
L8
M9
I-225
F3
M4
Evergreen
F1
Lakewood
M14
M3
P4
Morrison
L4
F5
F7
F2
Santa Fe Dr
Littleton
I-25
M11
M10
C-470
M5
L5
E-470
F6
285
Conifer
M17
Parker
L3
Lone Tree
Roxborough
Park
I-25
P6
L6
F4
Pine

Legend

P2 Prairie trails
M2 Denver Metro trails
L2 Lower Foothills trails
F2 Foothills trails

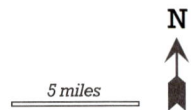

N

5 miles

page		park	trail	length (miles)	steepness	bumpy factor	gain (feet)
10	P1	Barr Lake State Park	Lake Perimeter Trail	9.0	▲	✿	20
14	P2	Rocky Mountain Arsenal	Ladora Trail loop	2.9	▲	✿	40
19	P3	Second Creek Open Space	Second Creek Greenway Trail	4.0	▲▲	✿	60
23	P4	Great Plains Park	Plains Trail	4.5	▲▲▲	✿	160
27 HM	P5	Ragweed Draw Open Space	Ragweed Draw Trail	2.6	▲	✿	40
27 HM	P6	Bingham Lake Park	Bingham Lake Trail	2.4	▲▲▲	✿	120
28	M1	City Park	Mile High Loop	3.1	▲	✿	50
32	M2	Washington Park	Outer Dirt Path Loop	2.6	▲	✿	40
35	M3	Cherry Creek State Park	Wetland Preserve Loop	3.1	▲	✿✿	50
39	M4	High Line Canal Trail	Cherry Hills/Greenwood section	4.7	▲▲	✿	60
43	M5	High Line Canal Trail	Littleton section	4.2 / 6.4	▲▲	✿	50 / 80
47	M6	Sand Creek Greenway	Star K Ranch section	3.8 / 5.8	▲▲	✿	70 / 100
51	M7	North Westminster Trails	Big Dry Creek Trail	6.1	▲▲	✿	100
55	M8	Crown Hill Park	Horse trail loop	3.3	▲▲	✿✿	60
59	M9	Quincy Reservoir	Gravel loop	4.8 / 3.1	▲▲	✿✿	40 / 100
63	M10	South Suburban Trails	Big Dry Creek Trail	4.0	▲▲▲	✿	140
67	M11	South Suburban Trails	Lee Gulch Trail	4.0 / 4.6	▲▲▲	✿	150 / 200
71	M12	Coal Creek Regional Trail	Louisville section	5.4 / 6.3	▲▲▲	✿	260 / 320
75	M13	Standley Lake Regional Park	Big Dry Creek / Dam Trail	3.4 / 4.0	▲▲▲▲▲	✿✿	260 / 280
79 HM	M14	Cherry Creek State Park	Cottonwood Creek Trail	3.8	▲▲	✿	60
79 HM	M15	Coyote Run Open Space	Harper Lake / Coyote Run	3.4	▲▲▲	✿	140
80 HM	M16	Colorado Hills Open Space	Westminster Hills Trail	2.3 / 4.2	▲▲▲	✿✿✿	150 / 260
80 HM	M17	Bluffs Regional Park	Bluffs Loop Trail	2.7	▲▲▲▲▲	✿✿	380
81	L1	Jeff Co Open Space	Fairmount Trail	5.5	▲▲	✿✿	110
85	L2	Jeff Co Open Space	Grant-Terry Trail	3.2	▲▲	✿✿	150
89	L3	Waterton Canyon	Waterton Canyon Trail	6.9	▲▲	✿✿	130
93	L4	Bear Creek Lake Park	Owl – Fitness Trail loop	3.1 / 3.7	▲▲	✿✿✿	100 / 150
97	L5	South Valley Park	Coyote Song / Swallow Trail	2.2 / 2.8	▲▲▲	✿✿✿	250 / 290
101	L6	Roxborough State Park	Fountain Valley Trail	2.6	▲▲▲▲	✿✿	300
105 HM	L7	City of Golden	Tony Grampsas Trail	2.6	▲▲	✿✿	120
105 HM	L8	Jeff Co Open Space	Lookout Mountain Nature Center	1.5	▲▲▲	✿✿✿	200
106	F1	Lair o' the Bear Park	Bear Creek Trail	4.1	▲▲	✿✿✿✿	250
110	F2	Mount Falcon Park	Castle Trail	2.7	▲▲▲▲▲	✿✿✿	400
114	F3	Elk Meadow Park	Painters Pause Trail	3.3 / 4.0	▲▲▲▲▲	✿✿✿✿	440 / 530
118 HM	F4	Pine Valley Ranch Park	Narrow Gauge Trail	2.0	▲▲	✿✿✿	100
118 HM	F5	Alderfer/Three Sisters Park	Meadow / Wild Iris Loop	2.0	▲▲▲	✿✿✿✿	150
119 HM	F6	Flying J Ranch Park	Shadow Pine Loop	2.8	▲▲▲	✿✿✿✿✿	270
120 HM	F7	Evergreen	Evergreen Lake Trail	2.5	▲▲▲▲	✿✿	80

▲ Steepness rating 1 – 5
✿ Bumpy factor 1 – 5
HM Honorable Mention

Introduction

Denver: a paradise for outdoor explorers

The Denver area boasts an average of 300 days of sunshine per year. With magnificent parks and spectacular open space systems, this is an ideal place for exploring off-road routes. There are more than 2,000 miles of trails within a short drive from the city, so the choices truly seem endless. Even within the city limits, one can find dozens of excellent soft-surface trails perfect for traveling on foot.

Trail running or hiking

Paved concrete paths are easy to find in Denver and are usually crowded, surrounded by urban sprawl, and anything but scenic. If you are not already a dedicated trail runner or hiker, here is a brief summary the benefits: because of increased shock absorption, soft surface trails are more forgiving than concrete or asphalt, resulting in fewer injuries. You breathe unpolluted air and receive shade from trees and other live vegetation. The sights, sounds, and smells of nature make trails interesting for kids and adults alike; exercising away from pavement and in green space is known to boost mental health. The constant slight changes in surface, elevation, and pace are better for your body. And instead of traffic and stoplights you will encounter wildlife and solitude. In the words of trail runner Steven Bragg (in his 2004 book *Run the Rockies*), "Once you try trail running, not only will you not go back to road running, but you may find yourself avoiding it at all costs."

Why this guide?

My wife and I love hiking, biking, running, and camping. In 2004, we moved to Denver to be in a place where we could be closer to outdoor opportunities. We purchased our first jogging stroller in 2008 and began running on unpaved trails with little Kenny in the stroller. The hardest part was finding suitable routes among the hundreds of trails in the greater Denver area; most trails in hiking books were too steep, narrow, rocky, or sandy. This guide is our attempt to share with you what we have learned over the years through trial and error.

These days, one of our family's favorite weekend activities consists of a stroller trail run or hike, followed by a picnic or some playground time (or both). The kids have gotten used to the idea of sitting still in the stroller for a 45 minute run as long as they are allowed to explore the outdoors afterwards. The main goal of this book was to introduce other active parents in the Denver area to the joy of running or hiking on unpaved trails. The routes in this guide were carefully selected for stroller use, with special emphasis on trailheads with picnic tables, playgrounds, and other interesting features.

The criteria for inclusion were simple: unpaved trails of at least 1.5 miles in length, wide enough for single and double jogging strollers, a gentle slope to avoid drastic elevation changes, and a minimum of rocks, roots, and ruts. The trailheads are located within 40 minutes (driving time) of downtown Denver, with the exception of a few honorable mentions in the Foothills section.

Most routes in this book can be run, walked or hiked, biked with bike trailers, or even accessed with wheelchairs. A quick scan of the trail descriptions will help you determine which routes are best suited to your favorite outdoor activities.

How to use this guide

The trails in this guide are organized into 4 color-coded chapters: Prairie, Denver Metro, Lower Foothills, and Foothills. Within each chapter, easier trails are presented first, while steeper routes are listed last.

Overview Boxes. Each trail description begins with five summary capsules with specifics for that route. Consult these first to get a quick idea of what the trail is like.

Length: The roundtrip distance of the featured trail from start to finish. If an optional trail extension or shortcut is included in the route, the alternate trail distance is listed second (for example: "3.2 / 4.2 mi"). All distances have been cross-checked with multiple maps and GPS data.

Steepness: The average vertical steepness of the trail (from 1 to 5). The flattest route in this guide is a "1" and the steepest is a "5."

Bumpy factor: This number (from 1 to 5) gives you an idea of how bumpy your trip will be. It's a subjective rating with a super-smooth trail rated "1" and a trail with lots of ruts or rocks rated a "5."

Trail surface: A description of the type of surface you will be traveling on, e.g. dirt road, forest floor, or gravel path.

Trail width: The narrowest and the widest section you will encounter along each route.

Trail condition: A summary of the trail surface and in what condition you may expect to find it. Examples include: mostly smooth, ruts, rocks, sand, or roots.

Starting elevation: The approximate elevation of the trailhead.

Elevation gain: The approximate gain in elevation throughout the entire featured roundtrip route (cumulative gain). If an optional trail extension or shortcut is included in the route, the alternate route elevation gain is listed second (for example: "470 / 600 ft").

Location: The city or municipality that the trailhead is located in.

Distance from downtown: The approximate driving distance, measured along the roads described in *Directions*, starting in downtown Denver.

Drive time: The approximate driving time from downtown Denver to the trailhead.

Access: A description of fees or permits (if any) needed to access the trailhead.

Trailhead picnic tables, restrooms, and water: Describes whether picnic tables, restrooms, and drinking water are available at or near the trailhead. Note that many restrooms and nearly all water fountains are closed in the winter months.

Playground: Notes if a playground is present anywhere along the featured trail route (or nearby).

Stroller type: Describes which types of strollers are recommended for the trail (such as off-road tires) and whether the trail can easily accommodate double-wide strollers.

Maps. Each featured trail is accompanied by a map. Its main purpose is to give you a sense of the general geographical layout as well as the location of any facilities. The following symbols are used:

P Trailhead Parking Lot

P Other Parking

Restroom

Picnic Table

Playground

Water

I-76 ———— Major Road or Freeway

———— Minor Road

→ Featured Trail

→ Optional Trail Extension or Shortcut

---------- Other Unpaved or Paved Trail

– · – · – · · Creek, River, or Canal

Directions. The driving directions provided are from downtown Denver.

Trail Description. This section guides you through the featured route. Points of interest and other important information is given from the point of view of a runner or hiker.

History & Info. Additional information about the trail, historical information, and other facts of interest are provided here.

Special considerations. This section covers regulations, restrictions, or other special information you need to know before you head out to the trailhead. It also lists park hours, if applicable.

Tips & suggestions

Tires. Using thorn-resistant tubes on your stroller tires is highly recommended; you will encounter drastically fewer flat tires. For our own strollers, I also applied a tube sealant (to instantly seal smaller punctures); it is sold in bottles under the *Slime* brand name.

Entry fees. Access to most trails in this guide is free. However, I recommend purchasing a Colorado State Parks annual pass for unlimited entry into all state parks. In addition to the four trailheads in this book that require state park access, you will be able to use the pass for hiking or other activities throughout the year.

Safety. Always stay in control of your stroller and walk steeper sections with caution. Visit at times when popular parks are not congested. Be prepared to take breaks, and bring snacks or other diversions for the kids on longer routes. Though young children are often soothed to sleep by the motion of running, jogging stroller manufacturers do not recommend running with an infant in a carseat adapter. And lastly, while all trails in this book have been researched thoroughly, the author assumes no responsibility for the risks inherent in hiking and trail running or changes in trail conditions or regulations. Be smart!

Thank you

The first print run of this guide was made possible through a crowdfunding campaign on Kickstarter (www.kickstarter.com). A very special thank you goes to all of my backers without whom the book would not exist. In particular I would like to acknowledge (in alphabetical order):

Heidi Camp	Erin Herlihy	Mike Patterson
Leeanne Coakley	Devon Jones	Erwin Sekirnjak
Rodney Devereux	Michael Kenney	Kimberly White
Tammy Downs	Heather Klof	Julie Zavala
Conor Flannery	Nancy Kruep	
Josh Gipper	Manpreet Mutneja	
Gerlinde Harb	Kathleen Noone	

Additionally, I would like to thank Julie Zavala for shooting several of the photos used in routes P1, P2, and P4. Manpreet Mutneja helped tremendously with proofreading. A huge thanks to my wife Debbie for her constructive criticism, running most of the routes with me, and proofreading the entire book. And lastly, big hugs to our kids, Kenny and Elena, who have patiently (and sometimes not so patiently) sat through all 145 miles of trails contained in this guide, multiple times over!

Barr Lake State Park
Lake Perimeter Trail

Length: 9.0 mi roundtrip
Steepness: ◢ 1 of 5
Bumpy factor: ✳ 1 of 5
Trail surface: dirt road
Trail width: 5-12 ft
Trail condition: smooth with an occasional rut or sandy section

Starting elevation: 5,100 ft
Elevation gain: 20 ft

Location: Commerce City
Distance from downtown: 26 mi
Drive time: 30 min
Access: $7 per car

Trailhead picnic tables: yes
Trailhead restrooms: yes
Trailhead water: no
Playground: yes

Stroller type: all types

Barr Lake State Park is located northeast of Denver and receives water from the South Platte River. The lake is owned and operated by an irrigation company and supplies water to farmers in the region as well as drinking water to local residents. The park is known as a prime bird-watching area: approximately 350 species of birds have been observed at Barr Lake. The perimeter trail encircles the entire reservoir on a wide, tranquil dirt road lined with cottonwood trees. You can easily run part of it and turn around wherever you like, or complete the full 9-mile loop. Please note that the segment of the trail crossing the dam remains closed during waterfowl hunting days. The trailhead parking area features a playground, restrooms, picnic tables, and a boat ramp.

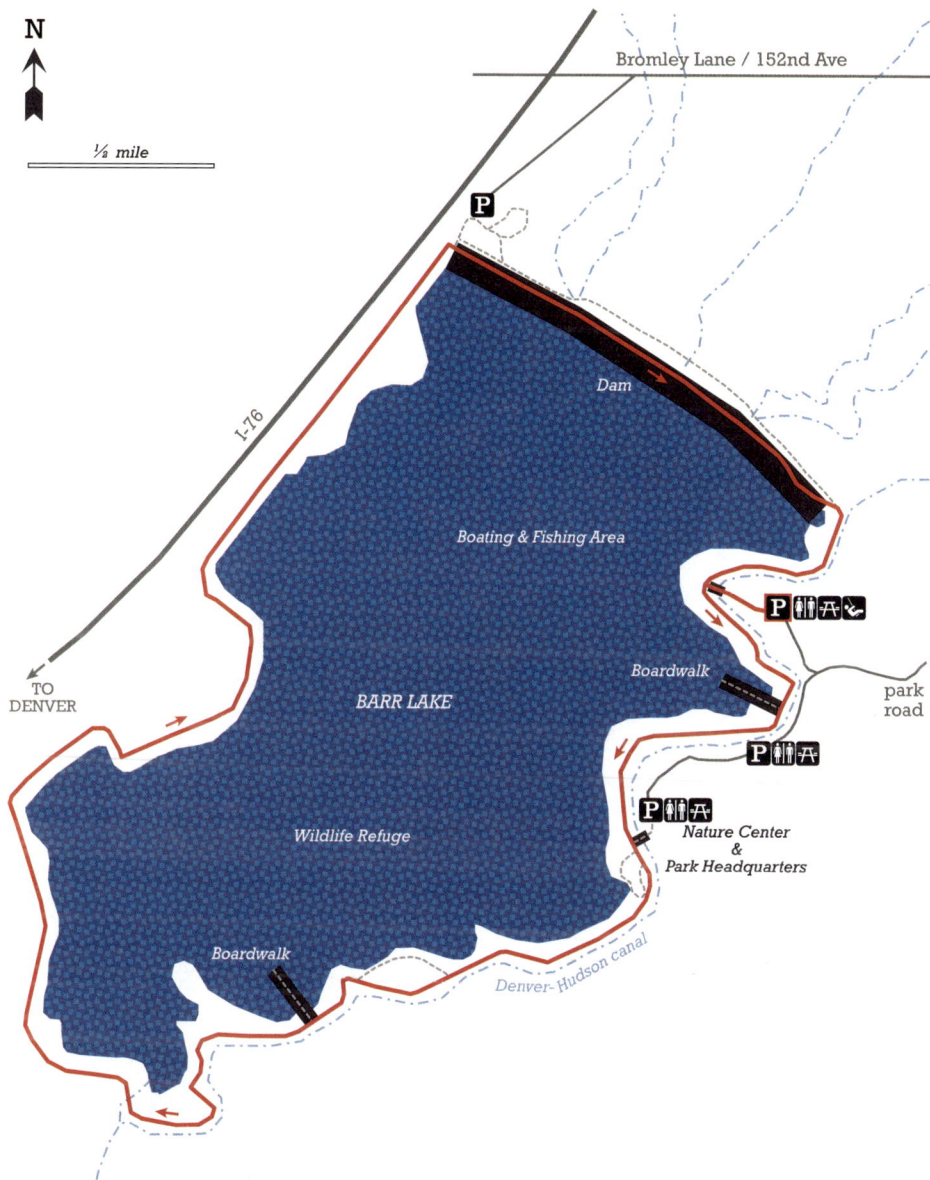

N

⅓ mile

Bromley Lane / 152nd Ave

I-76

TO
DENVER

P

Dam

Boating & Fishing Area

BARR LAKE

Boardwalk

park
road

Nature Center
&
Park Headquarters

Wildlife Refuge

Boardwalk

Denver- Hudson canal

Directions

Take I-25 north to I-76 (exit 216A). Take I-76 northeast and exit on Bromley Lane (exit 22). Turn right and go east for 0.8 miles to Picadilly Road. Turn right and go south for 1.9 miles to the park entrance on your right. Follow the park road past the entrance station. Turn right at the first junction, following the sign for the Boat Ramp. The road dead-ends at the trailhead parking lot.

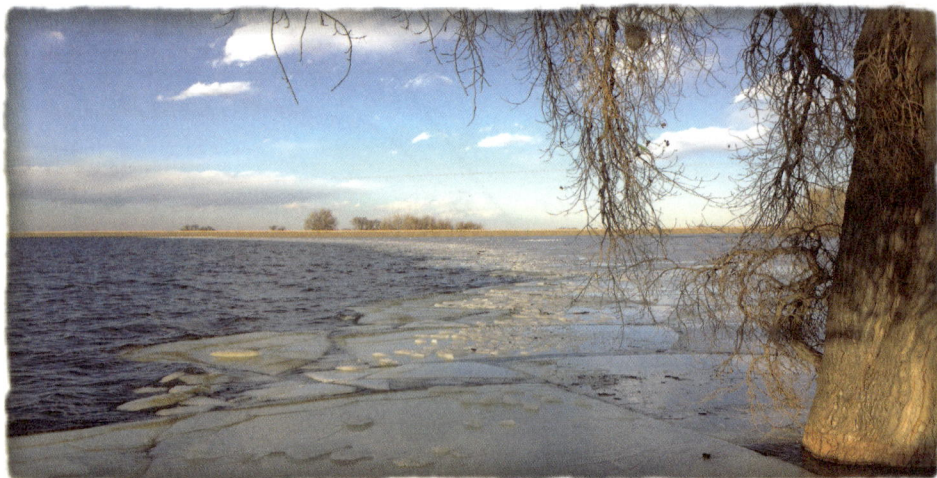

Trail Description

From the parking lot, run toward the lake, cross over a short bridge, and turn left to join the Perimeter Trail. The route described here follows the trail in a clockwise direction. The wide dirt road accompanies the historic Denver & Hudson canal half-way around the lake. A few side trails and two boardwalks within the first 3 miles beckon you to stop and explore. At 1.1 miles from the trailhead you will pass by a foot bridge leading to the Nature Center. At around 3.4 miles the trail veers to the right off the dirt road (follow the TRAIL sign), crosses a bridge and continues through marsh lands. This trail segment is narrower than the rest, but most strollers will fit on it. The trail then loosely parallels the nearby railroad tracks and I-76 for the next 2.5 miles before reaching the Barr Lake dam. Either turn right and cross the 1.3 mile-long dam (Crest Trail) or dip down to the trail below the dam. Then, turn right and follow the canal road back to the trailhead parking lot.

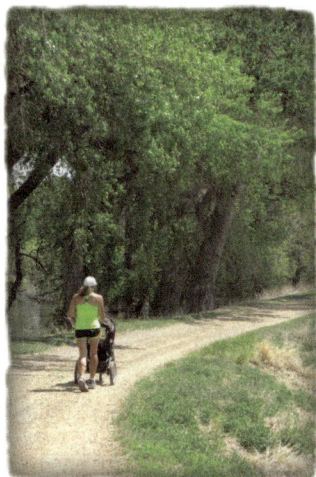

History & Info

In the mid-1800s, the area of present-day Barr Lake was a bison wallow, a natural depression in the prairie holding shallow water and mud. In 1886 the Burlington Canal was constructed to provide a stable

12

water source for settlers: water was diverted from the South Platte River into the wallow to create Oasis Reservoir. By 1890, the reservoir had become an elite fishing spot for Denver's anglers. In 1908 the irrigation company increased the size of Oasis Dam and gave the enlarged reservoir the name Barr Lake. Over the following decades, pollution nearly ruined the lake. For over 70 years, the reservoir was the downstream recipient of Denver's untreated wastewater. Finally, in the mid-1960s, clean water legislation and the flood of 1965 flushed out most of Barr Lake's pollution. Colorado State Parks was granted a recreational lease for Barr Lake State Park in 1975 and opened the park to the public in 1977. By the 1990s, the water in the lake was once again clean enough to be used as drinking water.

Special considerations

The trail across the top of the dam (Crest Trail) is generally open to hikers and bicycles, but is closed completely on waterfowl hunting days: Wednesdays and Saturdays from October through February (use the lower trail below the dam on those days). No swimming or wading is allowed in the water. Thorn-proof tires are encouraged because thorns are prevalent on the trail. Dogs are not allowed in the wildlife refuge area (southern half of the lake) and must be on a leash in all other parts of the park. The park is open daily from 5 AM to 10 PM.

Rocky Mountain Arsenal
Ladora Trail loop

Length: 2.9 mi roundtrip
Steepness: ◢ 1 of 5
Bumpy factor: ✿ 1 of 5
Trail surface: gravel & dirt road, short paved road sections
Trail width: 5 - 10 ft
Trail condition: mostly smooth

Starting elevation: 5,220 ft
Elevation gain: 40 ft

Location: Commerce City
Distance from downtown: 13 mi
Drive time: 30 min
Access: free

Trailhead picnic tables: yes
Trailhead restrooms: yes
Trailhead water: no
Playground: no

Stroller type: all types

Rocky Mountain Arsenal National Wildlife Refuge is one of the largest urban refuges in the nation. It is a sanctuary for more than 330 species of animals, including wild bison, deer, coyotes, eagles and owls. The Arsenal features approximately 15,000 acres of shortgrass prairie and has transitioned over the years from farmland to weapons manufacturing site to wildlife sanctuary. Since shade is scarce here, this route is ideal for a nature walk in the winter or fall. Make sure you take the kids to Lake Mary with its curved floating boardwalk and fishing platforms. Not far from the parking lot you will find a nice picnic area complete with views of the lake and an open meadow for playing.

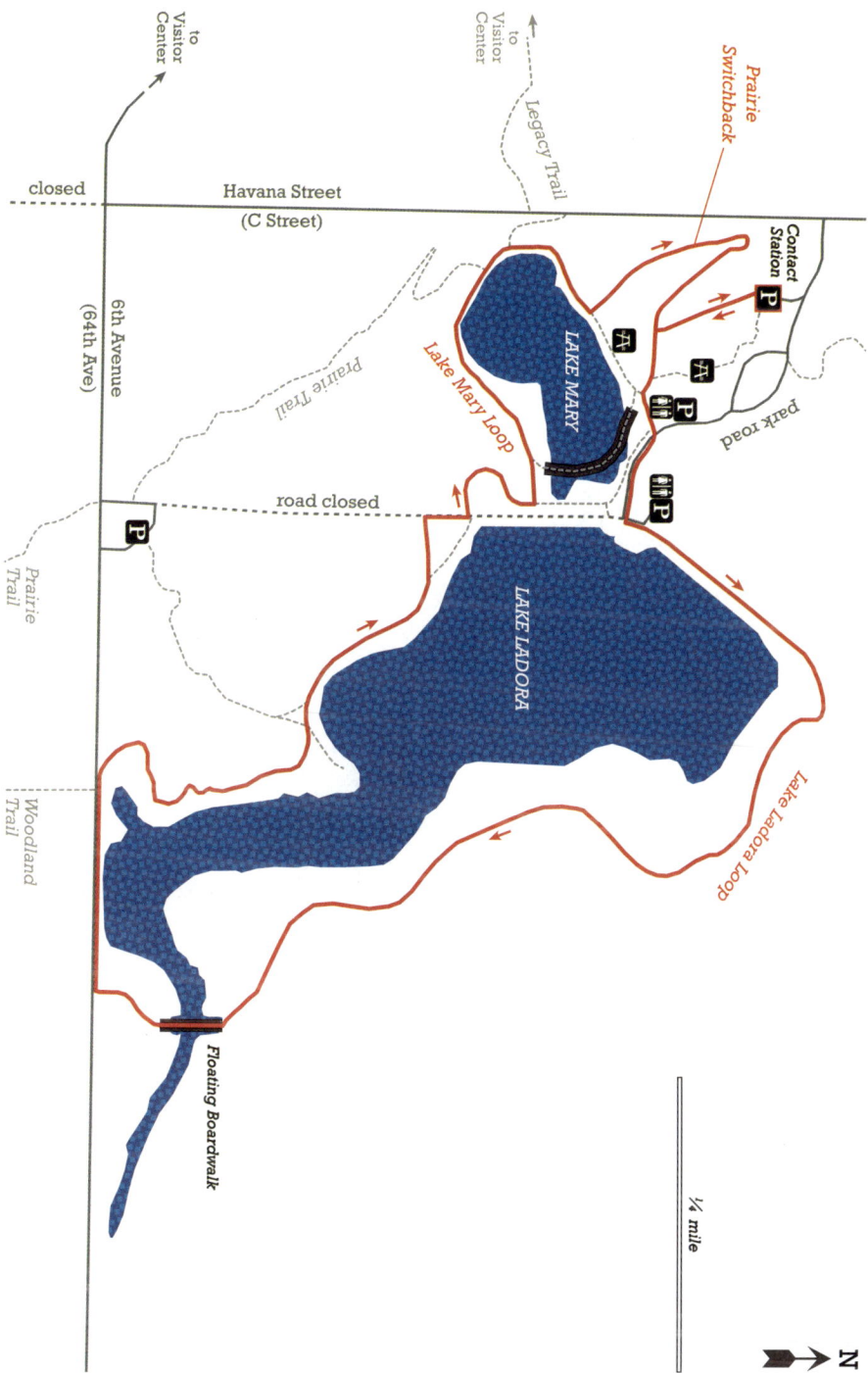

to
Visitor
Center

to
Visitor
Center

Prairie
Switchback

Legacy Trail

closed

Havana Street
(C Street)

Contact
Station

P

6th Avenue
(64th Ave)

A

LAKE MARY

A

Prairie Trail

Lake Mary Loop

P

P

road closed

P

Prairie
Trail

LAKE LADORA

Lake Ladora Loop

Woodland
Trail

Floating Boardwalk

¼ mile

N

15

Directions

Take I-70 East to Quebec Street (exit 278). Turn left and drive north on Quebec Street about 2.8 miles. Do not turn onto Northfield Blvd but follow Quebec to Prairie Parkway. Turn right on Prairie Parkway and travel 0.6 miles to Gateway Road. Turn left at Gateway Road and continue to the Refuge Entrance. Immediately after the entrance, turn right and follow the signs for the Contact Station (not the Visitor Center). After 1.2 miles turn left on Havana Street. Proceed 0.6 miles to the entrance for the Contact Station and park in the main parking lot.

Trail Description

From the parking lot, find the dirt trail leading down to picturesque Lake Mary. Pass the lake on your right and proceed to the paved park road. Turn right and follow the road up the hill to Lake Ladora. Turn left and begin a clockwise loop around the lake. You will encounter pavement for the first 1,000 feet as the road traverses the lake dam. After that, the route proceeds on a wide dirt path, winding its way along Lake Ladora's shoreline. Be on the lookout for deer, prairie dogs, and cormorants holding their wings out in the sun. About halfway around, you cross over a floating boardwalk, just wide enough for a double stroller. When the trail meets a paved road soon afterwards, turn right and proceed along the road for about 1,000 feet. Turn right again onto a dirt path (a "Lake Ladora" sign marks the way). The trail hugs the shoreline for half a mile before meeting another road. Turn right, follow the road for a brief 200 feet, then turn left on a path leading downhill to Lake Mary. Merge with the Lake Mary Loop Trail and follow it halfway around the pond in a clockwise direction. Just before the picnic gazebo, turn left and take the 0.3 mile Prairie Switchback Trail back to the parking lot.

History & Info

Early on, Indians lived off the land here as they followed bison herds. Later, settlers moved in and began raising cattle and growing crops. After the attack on Pearl Harbor in 1941, the U. S. Army converted the area into a chemical weapons manufacturing facility to support the war effort. During the Cold War, the Arsenal was used for the production of conventional and chemical munitions. In the early 1980s, an extensive environmental cleanup was begun by federal, state, and local regulatory agencies. Soon after, a roost of bald eagles (then an endangered species) was discovered, prompting the U.S. Fish and Wildlife Service to get involved. The discovery led to a congressional designation as a future national wildlife refuge. In the mid 1990s, a public-private partnership was created among the U.S. Army, Shell Oil Co., and the U.S. Fish and Wildlife Service. As the cleanup progressed, the Army transferred 12,500 acres to the Service to establish and

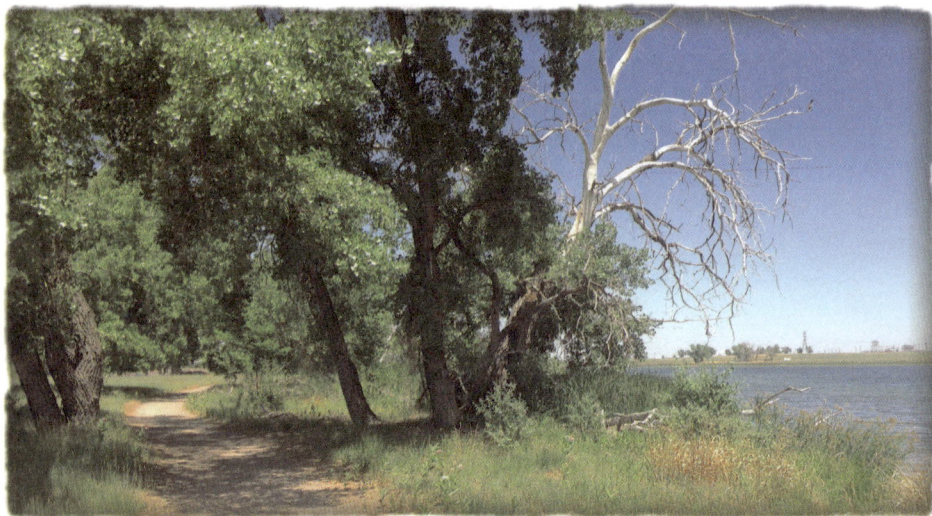

expand the Refuge. A small herd of wild bison was introduced to the refuge in 2007 (you may catch a glimpse of them in an enclosed area west of the Contact Station). The new visitor center opened in 2011.

Special considerations

Since this is a wildlife sanctuary, running is not encouraged here, so this trail is better walked as a nature stroll. Pets, bikes, and firearms are prohibited. Refuge hours are 6:00 AM - 6:00 PM, seven days a week, except for federal holidays. Visitor Center hours are 9:00 AM - 4:00 PM Tuesday - Sunday. Besides the featured Ladora Trail, the Refuge boasts several other trails worth exploring (such as the Prairie and Woodland trails).

Second Creek Open Space
Second Creek Greenway Trail

Length: 4.0 mi roundtrip **Steepness:** ◢◢ 2 of 5 **Bumpy factor:** ✳ 1 of 5 **Trail surface:** gravel & dirt path; short paved sections **Trail width:** 5 - 10 ft **Trail condition:** smooth throughout	**Location:** Commerce City **Distance from downtown:** 17 mi **Drive time:** 25 min **Access:** free
	Trailhead picnic tables: yes **Trailhead restrooms:** no **Trailhead water:** no **Playground:** yes
Starting elevation: 5,140 ft **Elevation change:** 60 ft	**Stroller type:** all types

Commerce City opened the Second Creek Trail in 2010, making it one of the newest additions to greater Denver's open space system. This route starts at Fronterra Village Park, which features a nice playground and picnic tables and is located less than ¼ mile from the greenway. The largely flat trail takes you through wide open grasslands and hundreds of prairie dog holes, following the banks of meandering Second Creek. Neighborhoods encroach on all sides, yet the atmosphere is tranquil and remote. You will find picnic shelters and a restroom along the trail; several bridges take you back and forth across the creek. If you want to skip the playground, you can park at the official Second Creek trailhead (Buffalo Mesa) and start this route from there.

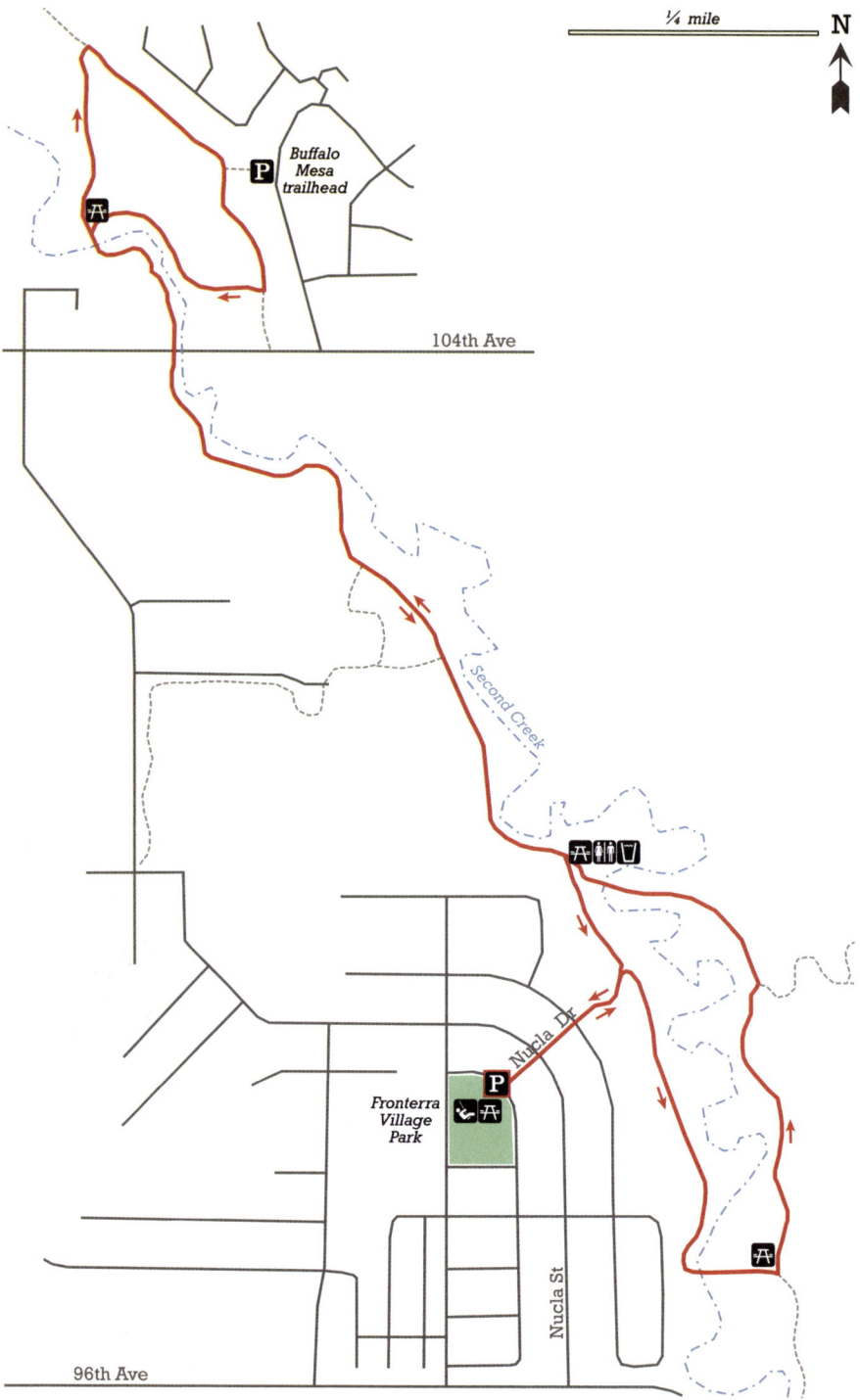

¼ mile

N

Buffalo
Mesa
trailhead

P

104th Ave

Second Creek

Nucla Dr

Fronterra
Village
Park

P

Nucla St

96th Ave

Directions

Take I-25 north to I-76 (exit 216A). Take I-76 northeast and exit at 96th Avenue (exit 11). Turn right onto 96th Ave East and drive for 5.6 miles. Just as the road dips downhill, turn left onto Nucla Street and drive for 0.3 miles. Turn left onto Nucla Drive. Park at Fronterra Village HOA Park (*16493 E 98th Way*). Alternatively, you can park at the Buffalo Mesa trailhead, located at *10480 Kittredge St.*

Trail Description

From Fronterra Village Park, use the sidewalk along Nucla Drive to connect to the Second Creek Trail (0.2 miles). When you reach the main trail, turn right and follow the south loop in a counter-clockwise direction. At the first picnic shelter turn left; the second picnic shelter along the route also features a restroom and water fountain. Proceed north along the banks of the creek and pass under 104th Ave. At the next picnic shelter keep going straight and enter the second loop (this one runs clockwise). Return along the creek and try not to miss the turnoff for the side trail to Fronterra Village Park. In addition to the gentle grade of Second Creek, there are only a few minor ups and downs along this route.

History & Info

Proposals for the Second Creek Greenway Trail were included in the Prairieways Action Plans of 1999 and 2005. The project was chosen based on local resident feedback, which ranked hiking and biking trails as a high priority in a 2007 survey. Commerce City began construction and the trail was completed in 2010. Today the trail connects to the Rocky Mountain Arsenal National Wildlife Refuge Perimeter Trail. In the future, the extended regional trail will eventually span 17 miles, from Brighton and Adams County south to Denver and Aurora.

Special considerations

The trail is open 5:00 AM - 10:00 PM. Pets must be on a leash. Motor vehicle access is not allowed. Fronterra Village Park has a meadow, playground, and picnic tables, but no restrooms.

Great Plains Park
Plains Trail

Length: 4.5 mi roundtrip **Steepness:** ◢◢◢ 3 of 5 **Bumpy factor:** ✳ 1 of 5 **Trail surface:** gravel & dirt road, short paved section **Trail width:** 6 - 9 ft **Trail condition:** smooth throughout	**Location:** Aurora **Distance from downtown:** 23 mi **Drive time:** 30 min **Access:** free
	Trailhead picnic tables: yes **Trailhead restrooms:** yes **Trailhead water:** no **Playground:** yes
Starting elevation: 5,670 ft **Elevation change:** 160 ft	**Stroller type:** all types

This trail follows the edge of the 1,100-acre Plains Conservation Center, an outdoor education facility and natural area. It is not a flat route but gently undulates across rolling hills. As there is no shade on this prairie trail, it is best avoided on hot summer days. You will see prairie dogs and catch some nice views of the front range mountains. The playground at Great Plains Park is fantastic; it has separate sections for younger and older kids and includes a spray-ground for cooling off on warm days. The nearby Plains Conservation Center merits an educational visit.

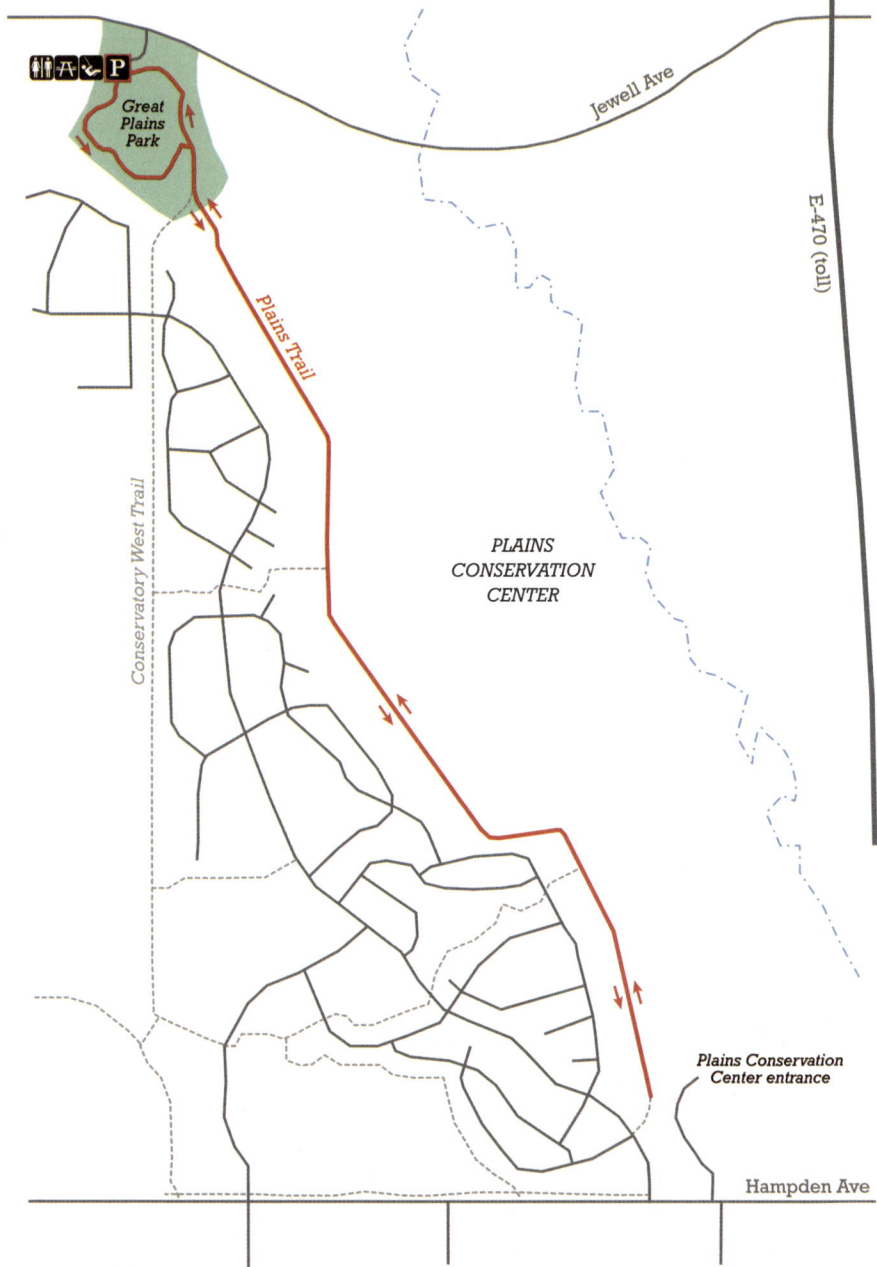

N

¼ mile

TO
DENVER

Jewell Ave

E-470 (toll)

Great
Plains
Park

Plains Trail

Conservatory West Trail

PLAINS
CONSERVATION
CENTER

Plains Conservation
Center entrance

Hampden Ave

Directions

Drive east on I-70 and take exit 289 to E-470 South (toward Colo. Springs). Continue south on E–470 (note that this is a toll road with automated license plate billing). Exit at Jewell Ave (exit 16) and turn right. After 1.5 miles, turn left into the parking lot for Great Plains Park.

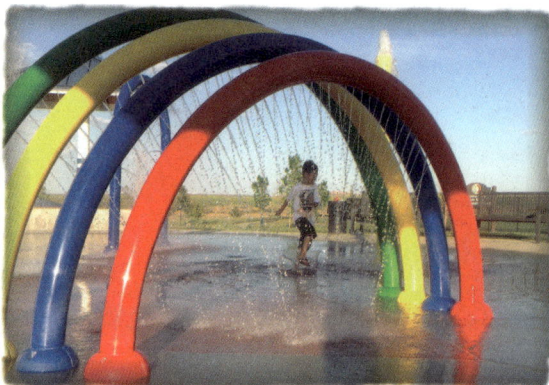

Trail Description

From the Great Plains Park playground, find the outer gravel path and circle counterclockwise around the park. When you encounter a paved trail, turn right and follow it for 1,000 feet to the Plains Trail entrance. Here, a wide dirt path leads you for 2 miles over rolling hills alongside a fence marking the edge of the Plains Conservation Center. At times you will travel near houses; at other times you are mostly surrounded by shortgrass prairie. As you near the turnaround, look to your left and glimpse Wells Crossing, a replica of a late 19th century farm. Turn around at the trail's end and return on the (mostly downhill) trail.

History & Info

The prairie ecosystem surrounding this trail resembles what you might have encountered here hundreds of years ago. Compared with the tallgrass prairie of central North America, the semi-arid climate of Colorado's shortgrass prairie receives far less precipitation. These rangelands were formerly grazed by American bison.

Special considerations

In addition to a playground, Great Plains Park also provides a baseball diamond, a basketball half court, a spray-ground, soccer fields, and a reservable picnic shelter.

P5 Ragweed Draw Open Space - Ragweed Draw Trail

Length: 2.6 mi. **Steepness**: 1 of 5. **Bumpy factor**: 1 of 5. **Trail surface**: gravel & dirt path; sidewalk sections. **Trail width**: 6-8 ft. **Trail condition**: smooth. **Starting elevation**: 5,050 ft. **Elevation gain**: 40 ft. **Location**: Commerce City. **Distance from downtown**: 15 mi. **Drive time**: 20 min. **Access**: free. **Trailhead picnic tables**: yes. **Trailhead restrooms**: yes. **Trailhead water**: yes. **Playground**: yes. **Stroller type**: all types.

Park your car at River Run Park in Commerce City, a sizable park with a nice playground. Connect to the Ragweed Draw Trail by following 115th Ave west until you reach the Open Space. The trail itself is a mere 1.8 mile out-and-back gravel route, partly following River Run Parkway. You will run through grassy meadows and around stands of trees. The trail is by no means remote, never straying too far from the houses, but it's a short flat route in a quiet suburban neighborhood.

P6 Bingham Lake Park - Pinery Loop / Bingham Lake Trail

Length: 2.4 mi. **Steepness**: 3 of 5. **Bumpy factor**: 1 of 5. **Trail surface**: gravel & dirt path, some paved sections. **Trail width**: 5-8 ft. **Trail condition**: smooth. **Starting elevation**: 6,150 ft. **Elevation gain**: 120 ft. **Location**: Parker. **Distance from downtown**: 30 mi. **Drive time**: 40 min. **Access**: free. **Trailhead picnic tables**: yes. **Trailhead restrooms**: no. **Trailhead water**: no. **Playground**: yes. **Stroller type**: all types.

This is a short but scenic high prairie route in south Denver. A playground with picnic areas are located at Lakeshore Park near the parking lot. Begin by following the Bingham Lake Trail in a counterclockwise loop around the tranquil lake (also known as Pinery Reservoir). Restrooms and picnic tables can be found halfway around the lake by the boat dock. After the 1-mile loop, take a right turn onto the last side trail before reaching the trailhead. This neighborhood trail adds a nice out-and-back excursion to your run, taking you uphill between stands of pines. The initial and final sections are paved; turn around when you reach Pinery Pkwy. The trailhead parking lot is located at *6045 N Thunderhill Rd* in Parker.

Denver City Park
Mile High Loop

Length: 3.1 mi roundtrip **Steepness:** ◢ 1 of 5 **Bumpy factor:** ✱ 1 of 5 **Trail surface:** gravel, crusher fines; several short sections alongside paved trails **Trail width:** 4 - 6 ft **Trail condition:** smooth	**Location:** Denver **Distance from downtown:** 2 mi **Drive time:** 10 min **Access:** free **Trailhead picnic tables:** nearby **Trailhead restrooms:** nearby **Trailhead water:** no **Playground:** nearby
Starting elevation: 5,260 ft **Elevation gain:** 50 ft	**Stroller type:** all types

City Park is the largest park in Denver and features a labyrinth of paved and unpaved trails and roads. The Mile High Loop follows a full 5 km (3.1 mile) route and tracks in part along the city's 5,280 feet (one mile) elevation contour line. 5280 markers indicate the points that are exactly a mile above sea level. The park also contains the Denver Zoo, the Museum of Nature and Science, two lakes, a historic boathouse, several fountains, flower gardens, and two playgrounds. Ferril Lake offers boat rentals in the summer and features the famous Prismatic Fountain, built in 1908. Note that for a park this size there is scant parking, creating traffic and parking issues on busy weekends. But since this is a loop trail, you can access it from any parking area in the park (or park on the perimeter streets near the park).

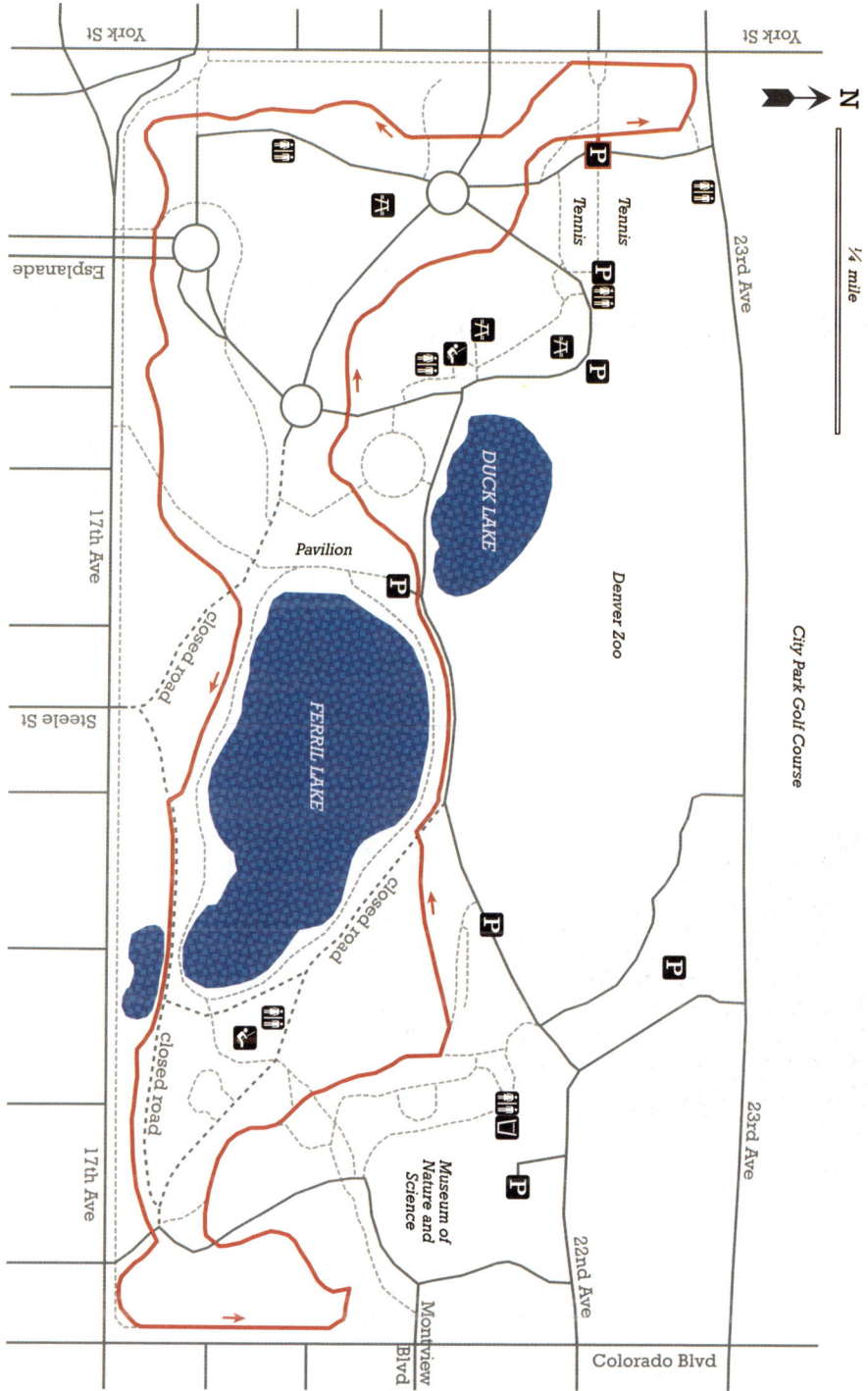

N

¼ mile

York St

York St

Esplanade

17th Ave

Steele St

17th Ave

23rd Ave

23rd Ave

22nd Ave

Montview Blvd

Colorado Blvd

City Park Golf Course

Denver Zoo

DUCK LAKE

FERRIL LAKE

Pavilion

Museum of Nature and Science

Tennis

Tennis

closed road

closed road

closed road

P

P

P

P

P

P

P

P

P

Directions

From downtown, take 17th St to 17th Ave. Go east on 17th Ave and turn left onto Downing St. Turn right onto 23rd Ave. Go east for 0.8 miles to the City Park entrance on your right, just past York St. Turn right onto the one-way road and park along the park road. There is additional parking in the lots behind the tennis courts, along the park road past Ferril Lake, or further up at the Denver Zoo / Museum parking lots.

Trail Description

This route begins at the north-west corner of City Park and follows the Mile High Trail in a counterclockwise direction. The trail is not hard to follow, except for a few sections alongside paved trails or roads. Its surface is small gravel or crusher fines throughout and takes you past several historic features as well

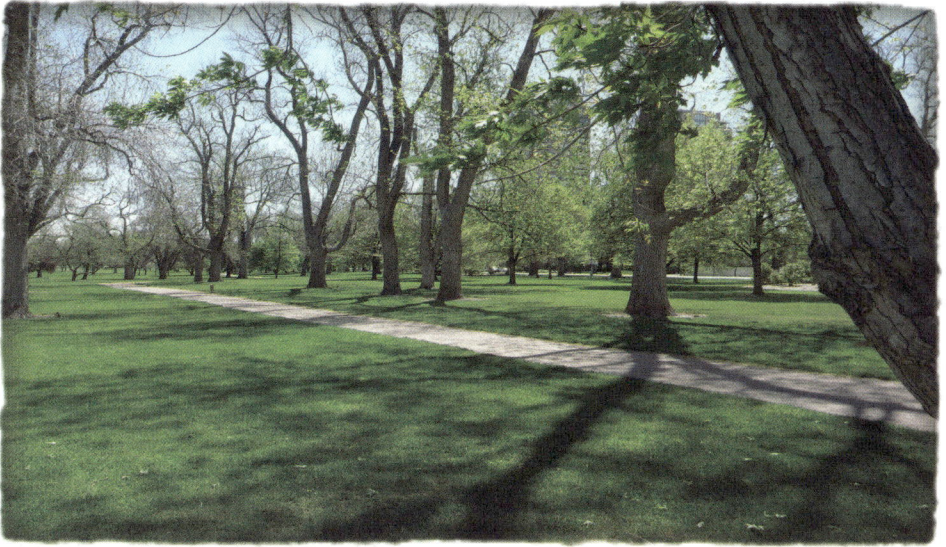

as some scenic spots. Two playgrounds (one large and one small) are within a short walk of the trail.

History & Info

In 1878, the Colorado state legislature passed a bill to permit Denver's acquisition of 1,280 acres of land for the construction of public parks. City Park became the largest tract turned into a park and green space. Ferril Lake and the Denver Zoo were added at the start of the 20th century, followed by the Museum of Nature and Science in 1908. The 3.1-mile gravel running trail was fully completed during the summer of 2009.

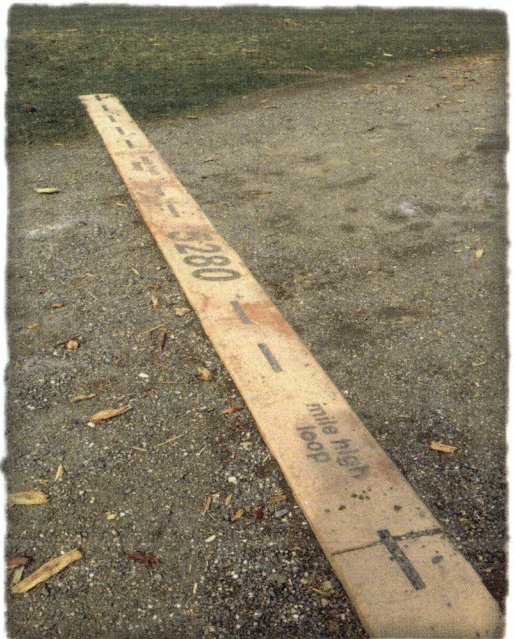

Special considerations

Denver Parks are open from 5:00 AM until 11:00 PM year round. Please do not feed the wildlife. Several restrooms in the park are seasonal, others are open year round. Often some part of the running trail may be be affected by construction or maintenance; please follow any detours provided.

M2
DENVER METRO

Washington Park
Outer Dirt Path Loop

Length: 2.6 mi roundtrip **Steepness:** ◢ 1 of 5 **Bumpy factor:** ✿ 1 of 5 **Trail surface:** crushed gravel and dirt **Trail width:** 5 - 7 ft **Trail condition:** mostly smooth	**Location:** Denver **Distance from downtown:** 6 mi **Drive time:** 15 min **Access:** free
	Trailhead picnic tables: yes **Trailhead restrooms:** yes **Trailhead water:** yes **Playground:** yes
Starting elevation: 5,310 ft **Elevation gain:** 40 ft	**Stroller type:** all types

This urban route is located in "Wash Park," a popular public park in Denver. It covers 165 acres, making it one of the largest urban parks in the city. The green space features several trails, including an inner paved loop (2.2 miles) and the outer unpaved loop featured here (2.6 miles). This trail is a gentle, crushed gravel and dirt loop that encircles the entire park. It is mostly flat with a few minor hills. The park has become a popular spot to enjoy nature in the middle of the city, especially in the spring and summer months. It can get very crowded on weekends, so come prepared to share the trail. The main playground, located near the parking lot, is large and almost always full of kids. Don't miss the boat and bike rentals on Smith Lake next to the boathouse during warm weather months.

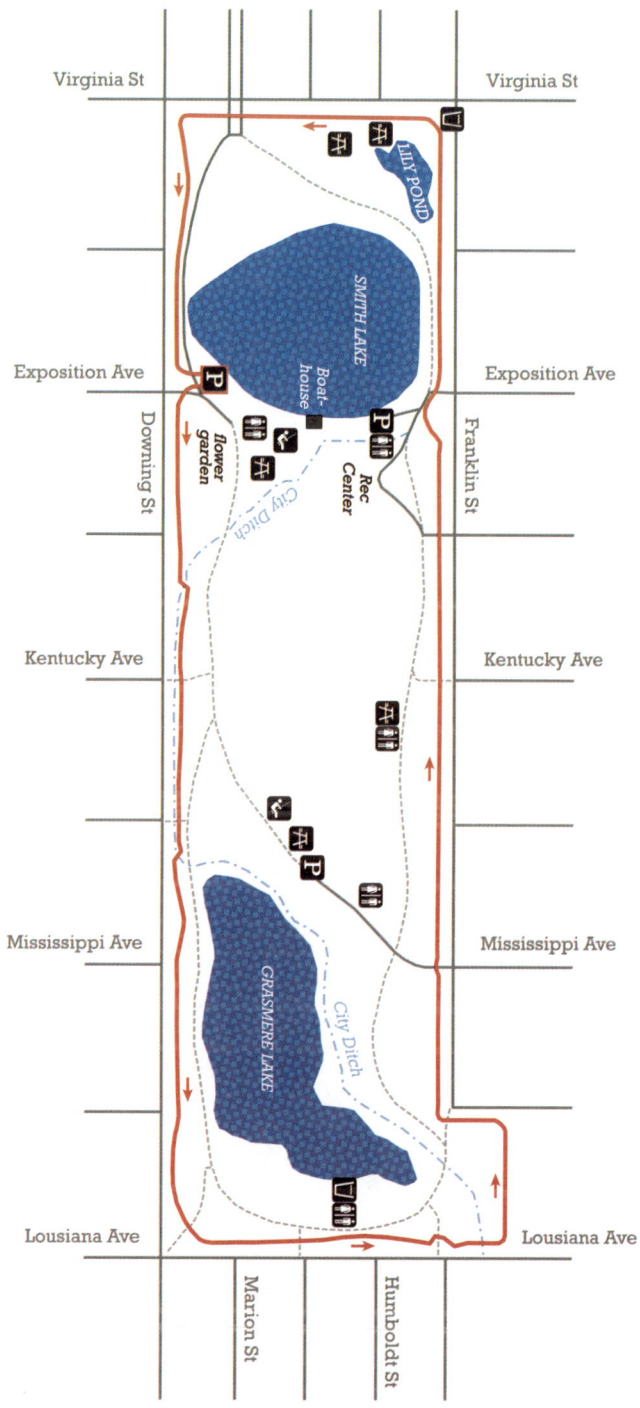

Virginia St

Virginia St

LILY POND

SMITH LAKE

Exposition Ave

Exposition Ave

Boat-house

Downing St

Franklin St

flower garden

Rec Center

City Ditch

Kentucky Ave

Kentucky Ave

Mississippi Ave

Mississippi Ave

GRASMERE LAKE

City Ditch

Lousiana Ave

Lousiana Ave

Marion St

Humboldt St

¼ mile

N

Directions

Take I-25 South to exit 206 (Washington St). Merge onto Buchtel Blvd, then turn left onto Louisiana Ave. Go straight on Louisiana Ave for 0.3 miles, then turn left onto Downing St. Go north on Downing for 0.8 miles. The park entrance will be on your right at Exposition Ave.

Trail Description

The route is straight-forward: you follow the unpaved path for a full loop around the park in a counter-clockwise direction. You will encounter shade trees, flower gardens, ponds, and grassy fields. One small hill takes you above Grasmere Lake, just enough for a scenic view of the park. If you need a longer workout, explore some of the paved trail options or run this route more than once.

History & Info

Wash Park was first developed by the German architect Reinhard Scheutze between 1899 and 1908. His original design has survived nearly intact to the present day.

The park's boat house was built in 1903 and boat rentals are still offered nearby. A landscape and structure preservation plan for the park was completed in 2011. Wash Park was designated as one of the "Great Public Spaces in America" by the American Planning Association in 2012.

Special considerations

Park hours are 5:00 AM - 11:00 PM. Other amenities include tennis courts, a lawn bowling field, two playgrounds, a rec center with an indoor pool, a flower garden, horseshoe pits, volleyball courts, and soccer fields.

Cherry Creek State Park
Wetland Preserve Loop

Length: 3.1 mi roundtrip **Steepness:** ◢ 1 of 5 **Bumpy factor:** ●● 2 of 5 **Trail surface:** gravel & dirt; some sand; short paved sections **Trail width:** 3 - 10 ft **Trail condition:** smooth with some rocks and ruts; a few boulders	**Location:** Aurora **Distance from downtown:** 18 mi **Drive time:** 25 min **Access:** $9 per car
	Trailhead picnic tables: yes **Trailhead restrooms:** yes **Trailhead water:** no **Playground:** no
Starting elevation: 5,590 ft **Elevation gain:** 50 ft	**Stroller type:** all types, but off-road preferred

This popular Colorado state park features a natural prairie environment with an 880-acre reservoir at its center. The park is used extensively by runners, cyclists, boaters, horseback riders, and campers. The route featured here has lots of twists and turns; make sure you study the map to avoid missing any turnoffs. It makes for an excellent hike and a very nice run. If you need a longer workout, try some of the other trails in the Wetlands area, or the 12 Mile Trail near the trailhead parking lot. The route requires a few short segments along the park road shoulder, but they are well worth it for the woodland tranquility that awaits you in the Wetland Preserve. More than half of this route is in the shade of large trees, providing relief from the sun in the summer. You will encounter a total of 4 wooden stiles, all wide enough for a double stroller to maneuver through.

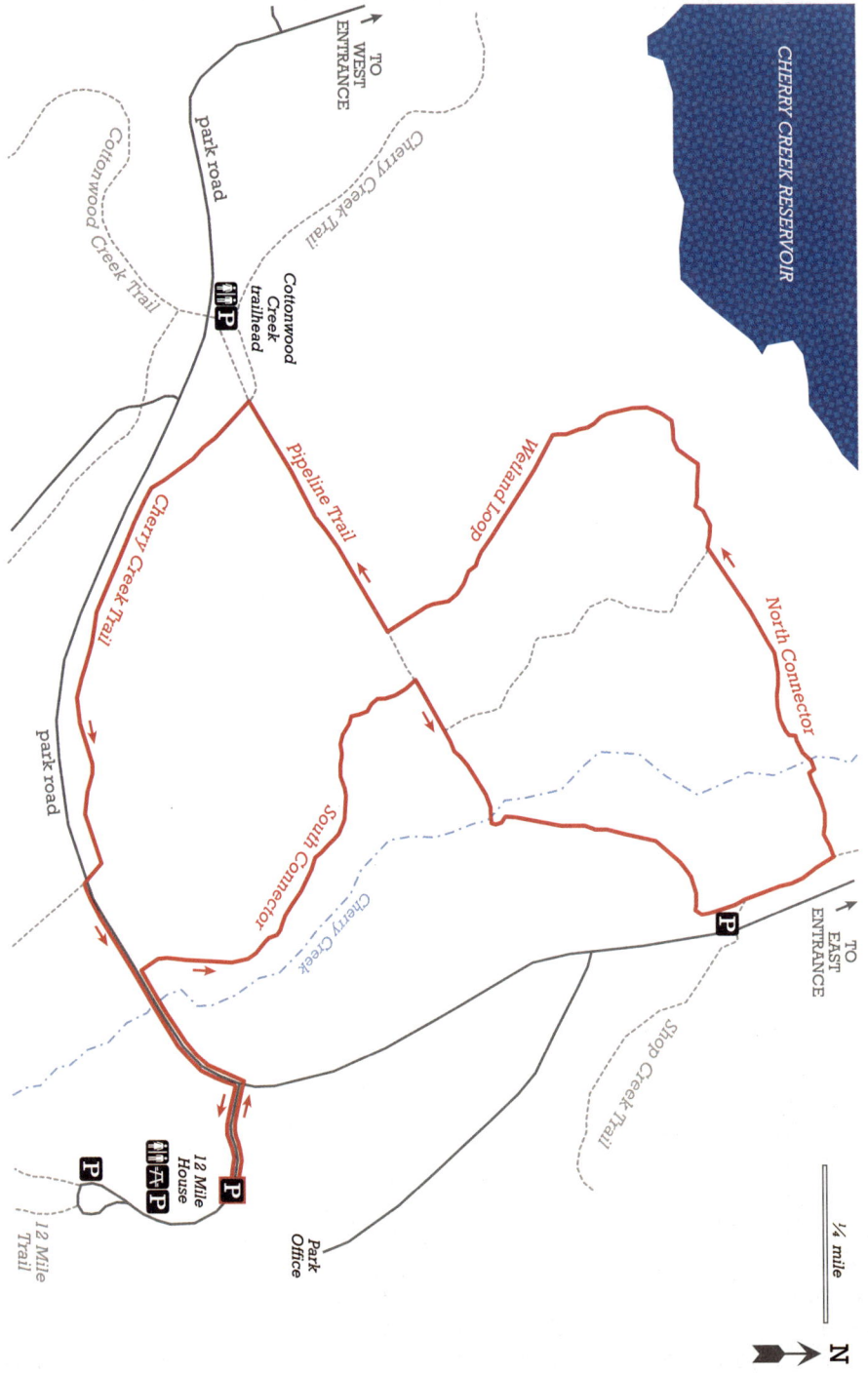

CHERRY CREEK RESERVOIR

TO WEST ENTRANCE

Cottonwood Creek Trail

park road

Cottonwood Creek trailhead

Cottonwood Creek Trail

Cherry Creek Trail

Pipeline Trail

Wetland Loop

North Connector

park road

South Connector

Cherry Creek

Cherry Creek Trail

12 Mile House

P

12 Mile Trail

Park Office

TO EAST ENTRANCE

Shop Creek Trail

¼ mile

N

Directions

Take I-25 South to I-225 (exit 200). Take I-225 North to Parker Road (exit 4). Turn right and follow Parker Road south for 1 mile. At the sign for Cherry Creek State Park, turn right into the East Entrance. After the entry booth, take a left. At the next intersection, turn left again. Proceed south on the park road for about a mile. Look for the "Twelve Mile Area" sign and turn left.

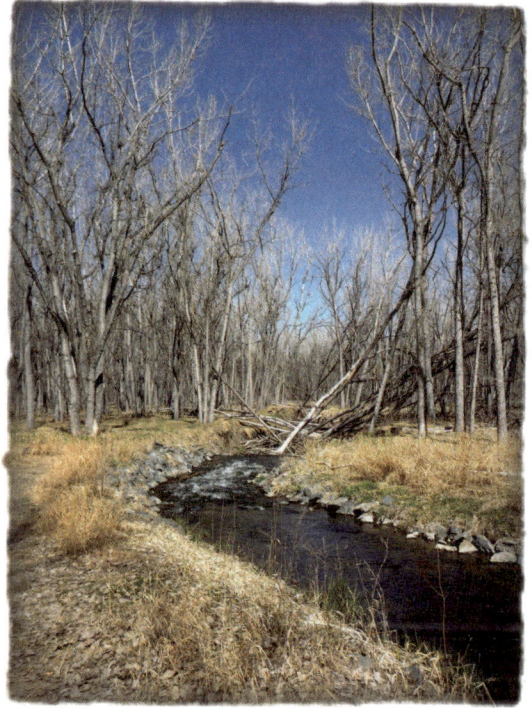

Trail Description

Begin by descending from the parking lot to the park road and turn left. Join the road cyclists and run on the shoulder of the park road for 750 feet. Shortly after crossing over Cherry Creek, find a trail on your right near a WETLANDS marker. This trail will lead you down into the wetlands reserve of the park. Cross a short 3-foot wide metal bridge, maneuver through a wooden stile, and enter the South Connector trail. At the junction with Pipeline Trail, turn right. Here the trail is at its widest. Soon after you cross over Cherry Creek on a foot bridge, you will cross an old abandoned paved trail. Boulders and rocks line this crossing - slow down to steer over them. After another stile, a gazebo, and a wooden bridge you pass by the Shop Creek parking lot on a

section of paved trail. About 500 feet past this parking lot, look for a gravel trail on your left. Here, turn onto the North Connector trail through another stile and re-enter the wetlands preserve. Cross Cherry Creek once again and proceed through a combination of forest and meadows. At the next intersection, keep right and complete the Wetland Loop. The last wooden stile brings you back to Pipeline Trail. Follow the wide path out of the wetlands area to the paved Cherry Creek Trail. Turn left and stay on the paved path until it crosses the park road. There, get on the road shoulder and make your way back to the trailhead parking lot.

History & Info

The Cherry Creek dam was built between 1948 and 1950 by the US Army Corps of Engineers to provide flood control as well as irrigation. It was the first of three dams to be built to protect the Denver region from catastrophic floods. You may find the following mammals in the park: cottontail rabbits, coyotes, beavers, muskrats, raccoons, weasels, prairie dogs, and mule deer.

Special considerations

No pets are allowed in the Wetland Preserve. Park hours are 5:00 AM - 10:00 PM daily. The park often reaches capacity on summer weekends. Entry into the park on busy days can include long waits at the entrance station; you may try the West Entrance instead - it is about the same driving distance to the 12 Mile parking lot as from the East Entrance. The Swim Beach area of the park has a small playground (but the Swim Beach parking lot is usually closed in the winter months).

High Line Canal Trail
Cherry Hills/Greenwood section

Length: 4.7 mi roundtrip **Steepness:** ◢◢ 2 of 5 **Bumpy factor:** ☉ 1 of 5 **Trail surface:** crushed-granite dirt road **Trail width:** 5 - 12 ft **Trail condition:** smooth	**Location:** Cherry Hills Village **Distance from downtown:** 12 mi **Drive time:** 20 min **Access:** free **Trailhead picnic tables:** no **Trailhead restrooms:** no **Trailhead water:** no **Playground:** no
Starting elevation: 5,480 ft **Elevation gain:** 60 ft	**Stroller type:** all types

Designated as a National Landmark Trail, the High Line Canal Trail runs alongside the High Line Canal, which delivers irrigation water to the city of Denver and communities to the east. The 66-mile trail from Waterton Canyon to the Green Valley Ranch area has become a major recreational resource as well as a fantastic way to see greater Denver. The trail segment featured here contains some of the most scenic stretches of the High Line Canal Trail, with a countryside atmosphere, panoramic Front Range views, and several open space nature preserves. Estates and villas dominate the landscape here, though it is mere minutes from the city's tightly packed subdivisions. The trailhead itself has no facilities, but there is a park with a playground less than 2 miles away (Eastmoore Park).

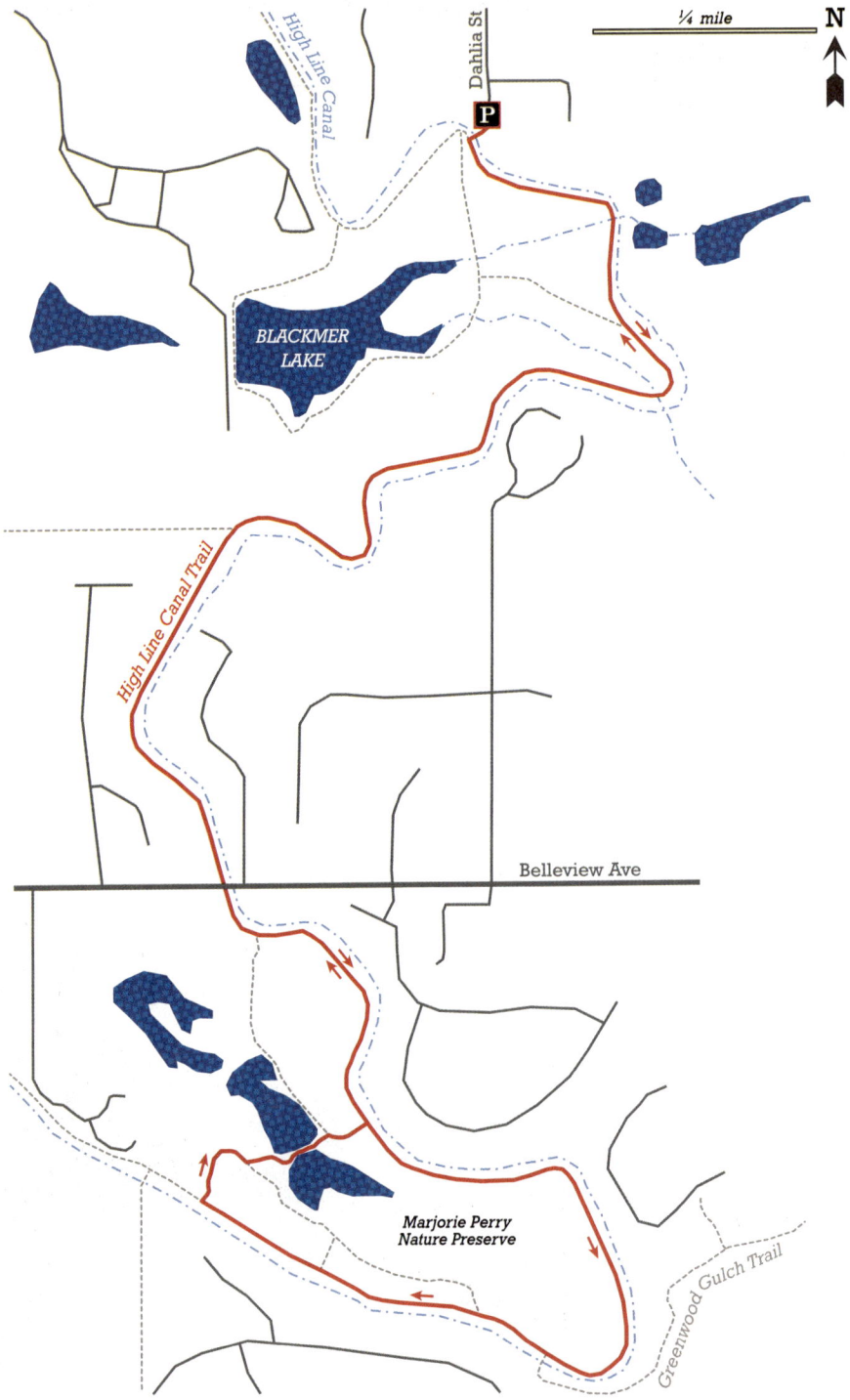

High Line Canal

Dahlia St

¼ mile

N

P

BLACKMER
LAKE

High Line Canal Trail

Belleview Ave

Marjorie Perry
Nature Preserve

Greenwood Gulch Trail

Directions

Drive south on I-25 and exit at Hampden Ave (exit 201). Turn right and proceed west for about a mile. Turn left onto Dahlia St. Drive south on Dahlia St for 1.3 miles until it dead-ends into a small parking lot.

Trail Description

Find the bridge across the High Line Canal and join the trail. Turn left and proceed along the wide dirt road for 2.7 miles. Enjoy the scenic views of lakes, meadows, and mountains. The upscale homes of Cherry Hills and Greenwood Village line the trail, but the atmosphere remains remote and rural. There are a few minor ups and downs; otherwise it's a very flat route. At the far end of the route you circle around Marjorie Perry Nature Preserve; look for a 5-ft wide dirt trail to your right. You will find it just before the blue house on your right and a bridge on your left. Leave the canal trail and turn right onto this side trail, proceed downhill and between two lakes. A short uphill section brings you back to the High Line Canal Trail. Return to the parking lot via the main trail.

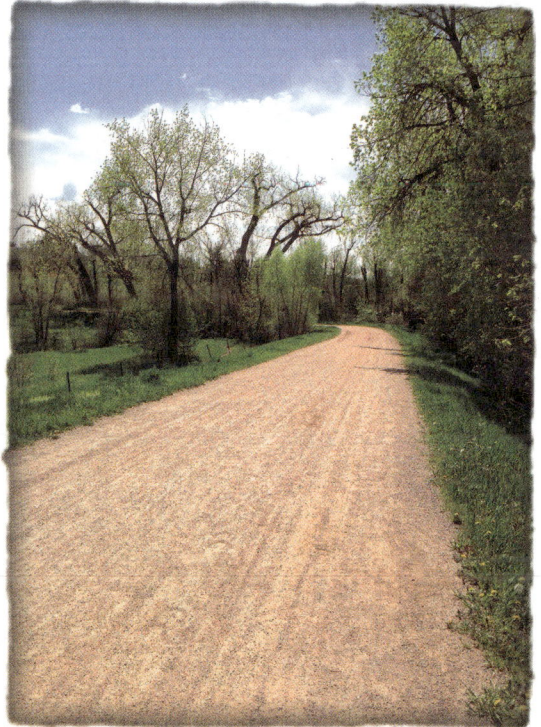

History & Info

Built by the Northern Colorado Irrigation Co., the High Line Canal was finished in 1883, transporting water from the mountains to the

prairie. Until 1970 the canal was closed to the public; now the path alongside it is designated a National Landmark Trail. The segment featured here is part of the first

portion to open to recreation. Today, hundreds of thousands of people use this section annually. The canal waters trees and plants, replenishes groundwater aquifers, and has effectively developed its own local ecosystem. In the past, High Line water in the south Denver area was used to irrigate fruit orchards, hay pastures, and alfalfa fields. Today, the canal is owned by Denver Water, and water flows in the canal sporadically from April to October.

Special considerations

No motorized vehicles are allowed. The canal water depth ranges from 2 to 7 feet. Swimming, tubing, and boating are strictly prohibited. The trail is open daily from 6:00 AM to 11:00 PM. Pets must be on a leash.

High Line Canal Trail
Littleton section

Length: 4.2 / 6.4 mi roundtrip **Steepness:** ◢◢ 2 of 5 **Bumpy factor:** ✲ 1 of 5 **Trail surface:** crushed-granite, a few brief paved sections **Trail width:** 8 - 12 ft **Trail condition:** smooth	**Location:** Littleton **Distance from downtown:** 14 mi **Drive time:** 25 min **Access:** free
	Trailhead picnic tables: yes **Trailhead restrooms:** yes **Trailhead water:** yes **Playground:** yes
Starting elevation: 5,530 ft **Elevation gain:** 50 / 80 ft	**Stroller type:** all types

The wide dirt road following the High Line Canal is a quiet retreat from the suburban sprawl of south Denver. The canal stretches across 66 miles from foothills to prairie. The trail surface of the segment featured here is a crushed-granite base (other sections of the trail are paved). The route begins at Writer's Vista Park, a

lovely park overlooking McLellen Reservoir with restrooms, a playground, and mountain views. The main route heads north for 2.1 miles to the junction with the Lee Gulch Trail (of course you can turn back at any point or continue further on). The optional route extension takes you south from the trailhead along the verdant banks of McLellen Reservoir for a little over a mile. The trail is flat except for a few short hills; watch for bicycles, horses, and people walking their dogs.

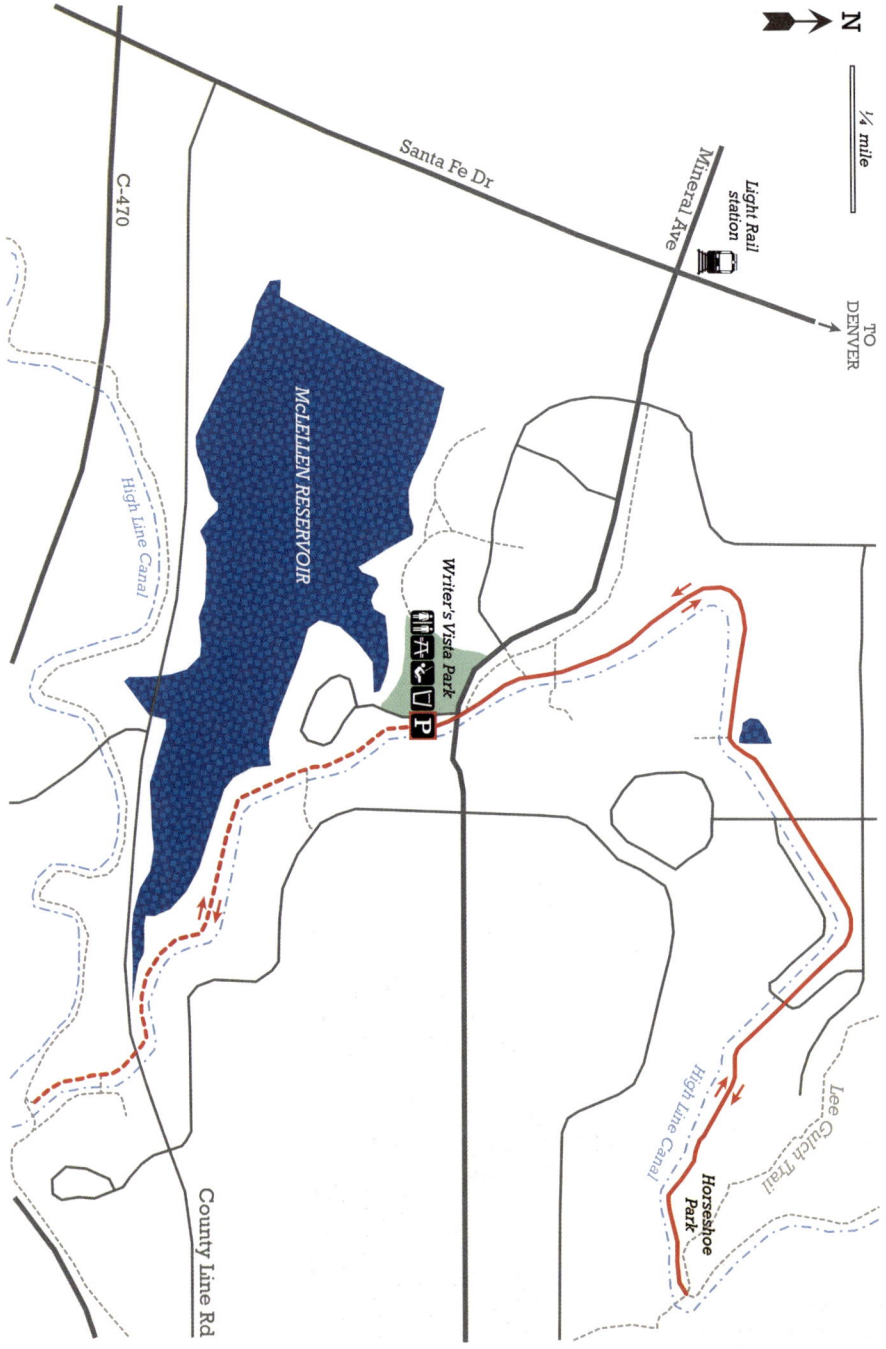

N

¼ mile

Santa Fe Dr

C-470

Mineral Ave

Light Rail
station

TO
DENVER

McLELLEN RESERVOIR

High Line Canal

Writer's Vista Park

County Line Rd

High Line Canal

Lee Gulch Trail

Horseshoe
Park

Directions

Drive south on I-25, take exit 207B, and proceed south on Santa Fe Drive (US-85) for 9 miles. Turn left onto Mineral Ave. Continue for 1 mile to Writer's Vista Park on your right (S Peninsula Drive). The trailhead is located about 1 mile from the Littleton/Mineral Ave light rail station (C/D line).

Trail Description

From the parking lot at Writer's Vista Park, turn left and cross Mineral Ave at the crosswalk signal. Proceed along the High Line Canal Trail for just over 2 miles through the neighborhoods of Southbridge, Bel-Vue Heights, and Littleton. The setting is semi-rural; you will see small farms, horses, and elaborate gardens. There are two minor street crossings. The large cottonwood trees in this section likely date back to the canal's earliest days in the 1880s. Turn around where the trail dips downhill and intersects with the Lee Gulch Trail (Horseshoe Park). For the optional extension, follow the High Line Canal Trail back to the trailhead and then beyond it for about a mile. McLellen Reservoir below the trail provides drinking water to the city of Englewood. Turn back where the gravel road meets the Centennial Trail and changes to a paved bike path.

History & Info

The canal was built in the 1880s to supply the dry prairie with mountain water, but the leaky canal never provided sufficient water for farming. Until 1970 the canal was off limits to the public; now the canal trail is a popular recreational pathway for non-motorized use. At the trailhead for this route, water in the canal has traveled approximately 24 hours from its origin in Waterton Canyon. For further information on the High Line Canal Trail, please see the History & Info section for route M4.

Special considerations

The canal water depth ranges from 2 to 7 feet. Swimming, tubing, and boating are strictly prohibited. The trail is open daily from 6:00 AM to 11:00 PM. Pets must be on a leash.

Sand Creek Greenway
Star K Ranch section

Length: 3.8 / 5.8 mi roundtrip **Steepness:** ◢◢ 2 of 5 **Bumpy factor:** ❋ 1 of 5 **Trail surface:** crusher fine gravel and dirt; short paved sections **Trail width:** 8 - 10 ft **Trail condition:** smooth with occasional ruts	**Location:** Aurora **Distance from downtown:** 14 mi **Drive time:** 20 min **Access:** free **Trailhead picnic tables:** yes **Trailhead restrooms:** yes **Trailhead water:** yes **Playground:** no
Starting elevation: 5,380 ft **Elevation gain:** 70 / 100 ft	**Stroller type:** all types

"Wilderness In The City" is the official slogan of Sand Creek Regional Greenway. And this section of the 14 mile-long public trail showcases its motto perfectly: it's an idyllic setting with little or no city noise, tall cottonwood trees, grasslands, and horse trails. The route featured here is at the eastern, upstream end of the Sand Creek Trail, arguably the most scenic portion of the Greenway. It starts at the Morrison Nature Center, a remodeled 1940s homestead on the Star K Ranch, now an outdoor wildlife learning center. The wide trail loosely follows the creek on a gentle slope with some minor hills. It is largely located within the 200-acre Star K nature preserve. The main route is a 3.8 mile out-and-back excursion, with an optional two-mile extension alongside the creek.

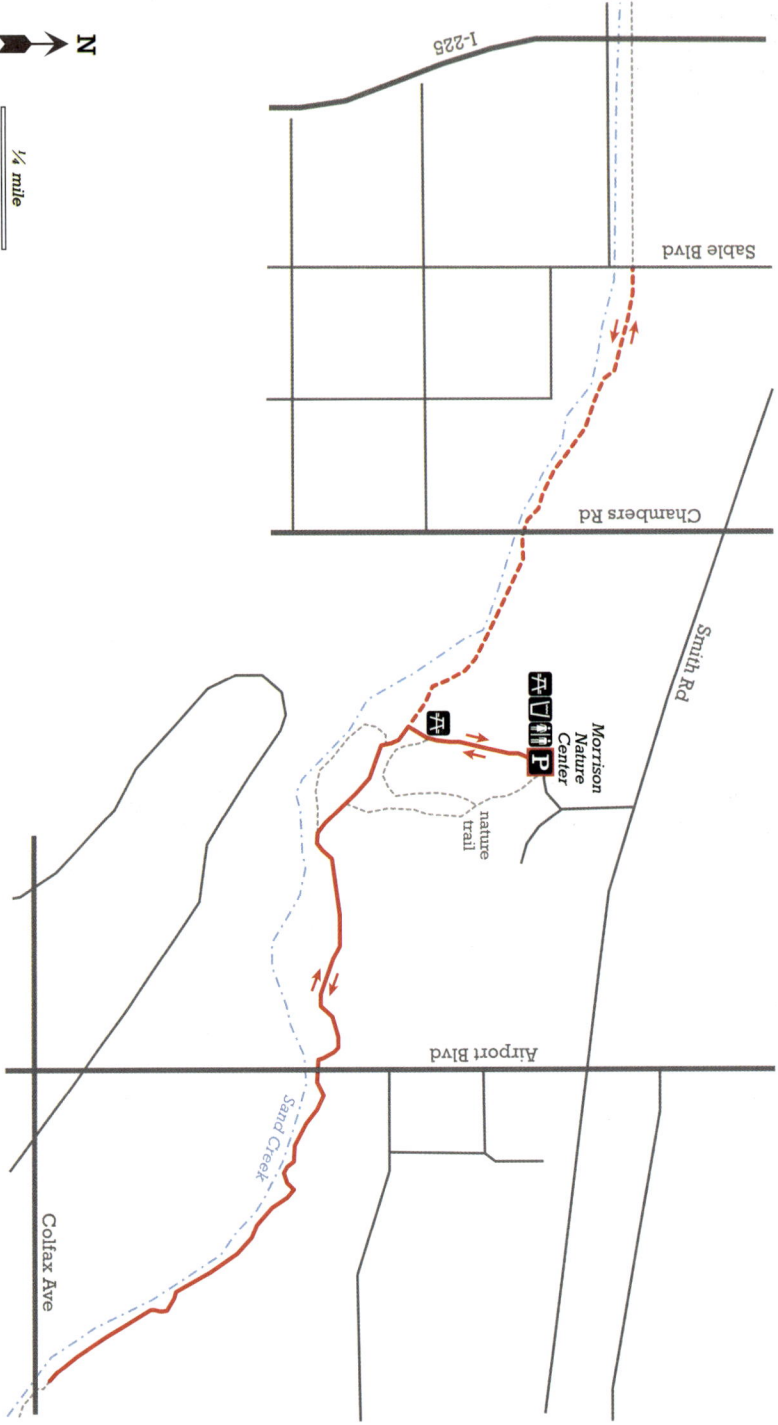

N

¼ mile

I-225

Sable Blvd

Chambers Rd

Smith Rd

Morrison
Nature
Center

nature
trail

Airport Blvd

Sand Creek

Colfax Ave

Directions

Take I-70 east to Chambers Rd (exit 283). Turn right and drive south on Chambers Rd, then turn left onto Smith Rd. After about half a mile, turn right onto Laredo St. Keep right and follow the signs to Star K Ranch. Park at the Morrison Nature Center, to your left.

Trail Description

From the Morrison Nature Center, begin at the trail near the outhouse. Join the Sand Creek Trail after about ¼ mile, shortly past a large picnic shelter. Turn left and

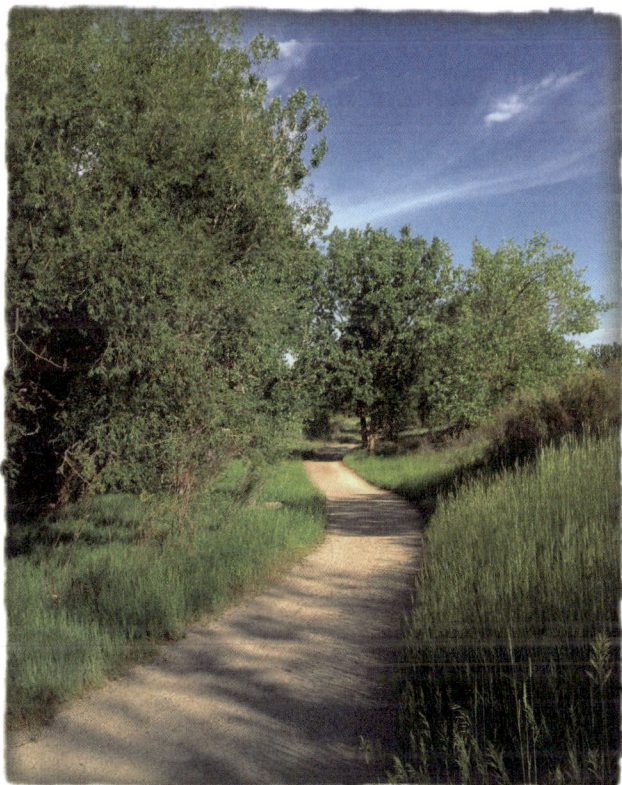

proceed for about 1.6 miles to the turnaround point. You will encounter a combination of meadows, groups of cottonwoods, and tree-lined creekside. Several short hilly sections will take you above Sand Creek. The maintained trail ends at Colfax Ave (a future eastward trail extension to the Aurora Reservoir is planned). Turn around and retrace your steps. For an optional extension, continue past the Nature Center turnoff. Here, the route closely follows Sand Creek, running alongside somewhat industrial neighborhoods. After about a mile, turn back at Sable Blvd, where the trail turns into a paved sidewalk.

History & Info

The Sand Creek Trail is one of the newest Denver area recreational greenways. The route was planned and construction began in the late 1990s, but it is still an unfinished project. The greenway currently connects Aurora to the South Platte River Greenway in Commerce City.

Animals frequently seen in the Star K Ranch area include mule deer, painted turtles, red-tailed hawks, American kestrels, and great horned owls. The free Morrison Nature Center is open Wednesdays to Sundays and well worth a visit. It features exhibits, restrooms, water, and picnic tables behind the building. A large picnic shelter is located less than ¼ mile from the trailhead (see map). A short nature trail loop starts and ends at the Nature Center.

Special considerations

The trail is open daily, dawn to dusk. Share the trail and be courteous to others (horses are permitted here). Keep pets on leashes, and clean up after them. The following are prohibited: weapons of any sort, drugs and alcoholic beverages, swimming or tubing, and glass bottles or containers.

Length: 6.1 mi roundtrip **Steepness:** ▲▲ 2 of 5 **Bumpy factor:** ❋ 1 of 5 **Trail surface:** gravel & dirt road, several short paved sections **Trail width:** 6 - 9 ft **Trail condition:** smooth with occasional ruts	**Location:** Westminster **Distance from downtown:** 14 mi **Drive time:** 20 min **Access:** free
	Trailhead picnic tables: yes **Trailhead restrooms:** yes **Trailhead water:** yes **Playground:** yes
Starting elevation: 5,190 ft **Elevation gain:** 100 ft	**Stroller type:** all types

This route connects two large Westminster playgrounds, so you may want to run it as two 3-mile legs with a play time stop in between. It follows Big Dry Creek Trail, the crown jewel of Westminster's extensive off-road trail system. You will encounter gently rolling hills and wide open prairie as you accompany Big Dry Creek on its way toward the South Platte River. Some trail sections feature wetlands and several small ponds. However, since the trail mostly traverses native grasslands, there is very little shade. The route featured here largely follows the main trail except for a shortcut in the first mile to circumvent a hill.

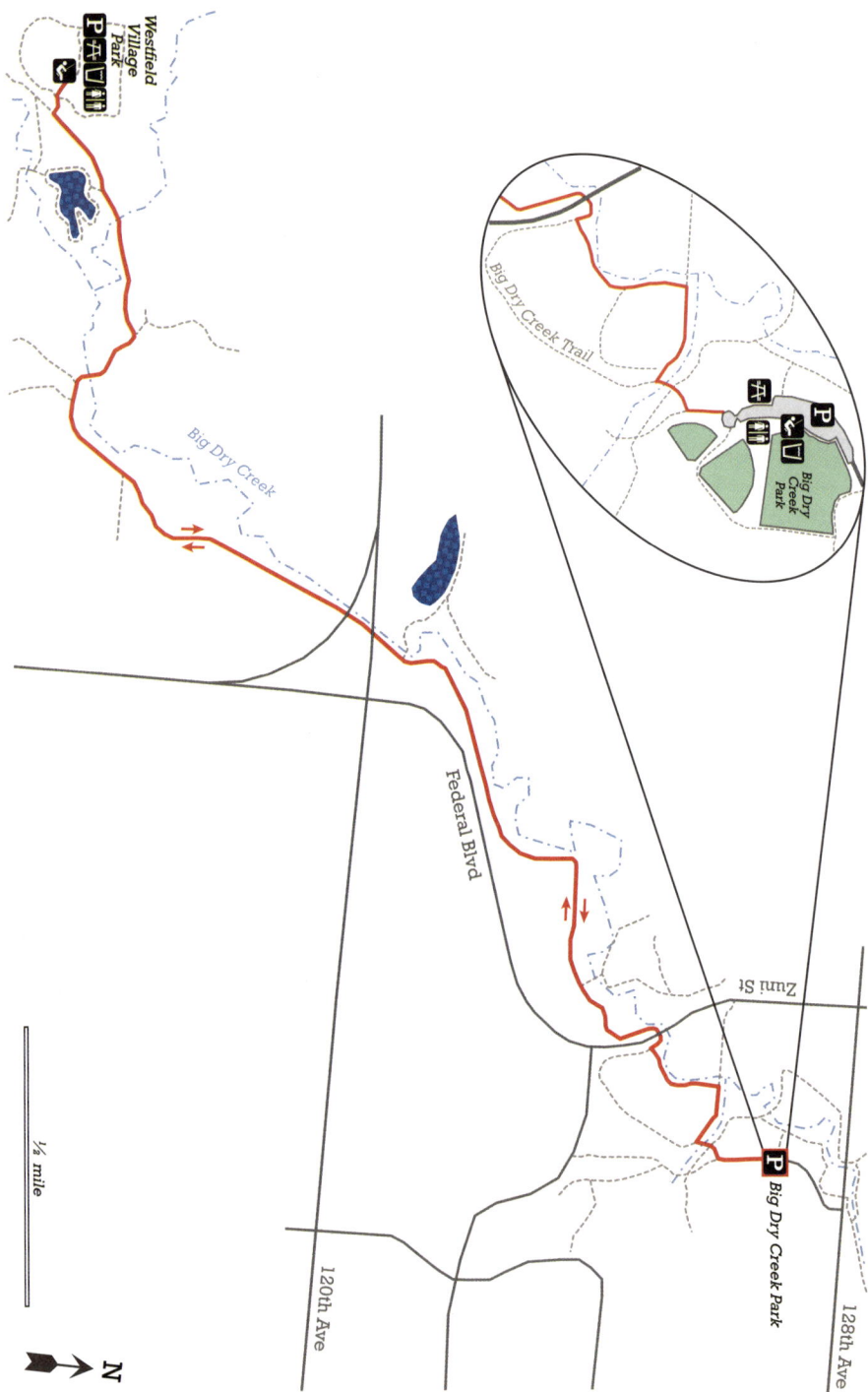

Westfield
Village
Park

P 🅰 🗑 📷 🚻

Big Dry Creek

Federal Blvd

120th Ave

Zuni St

128th Ave

P Big Dry Creek Park

Big Dry Creek Trail

🅰

P 🗑 📷 🚻 🚶

Big Dry
Creek
Park

½ mile

N

Directions

Take I-25 North to 120th Avenue (exit 223) and turn left. Go west for half a mile, then turn right onto Huron Street. After 1 mile, turn left onto 128th Ave and continue west for half a mile. The entrance to Big Dry Creek Park is on your left (and easy to miss); park near the playground.

Trail Description

Leave the park on the paved trail at the south end of the parking lot. As the trail turns into a dirt path, turn right, pass through a wooden fence, and descend into a tree-lined creek crossing (ignore the confusing trail sign). As you come up on the other side, immediately turn right (if you miss this turn and stay on the main trail, you will end up on the correct route but will add a significant hill to your run). After 0.1 miles, veer left (don't cross over the bridge) and follow along the creek. Turn right as you join Big Dry Creek Trail on a brief paved section and cross under Zuni Street. From here, stay on Big Dry Creek Trail whenever you see a side trail. At times the corridor follows the tree-lined creek valley, at other times it traverses wide open areas. Look for coyotes and foxes, especially at dusk. About 0.6 miles after crossing Big

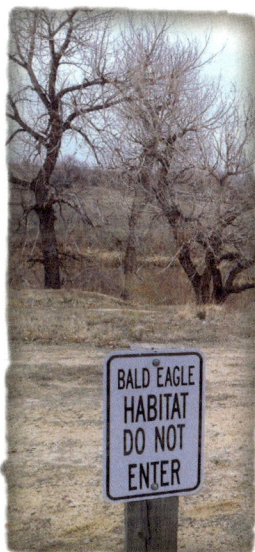

Dry Creek you will see the batting cages of Westfield Village Park in the distance to your right. Turn off the trail and aim for the playground. When the kids have had enough, get back on the main trail for your second 5k back to the starting point (mostly downhill).

History & Info

Big Dry Creek has long been part of a network of irrigation canals providing mountain water to the plains. As homes replaced farmland, most irrigation ditches were abandoned. The open space trail system now in place provides recreational opportunities such as hiking, fishing, and wildlife watching. The 12 mile long Big Dry Creek Trail was designated a National Recreation Trail in 2003.

Special considerations

Dogs must be on a leash. Please observe all "Do Not Enter" signs. Big Dry Creek Park at the trailhead provides a wide variety of facilities in addition to the playground, including a dog park, picnic shelters, as well as softball and soccer fields.

M8

DENVER METRO

Crown Hill Park
Horse trail loop

Length: 3.3 mi roundtrip **Steepness:** ◢◢ 2 of 5 **Bumpy factor:** ●● 2 of 5 **Trail surface:** gravel path; very short paved sections **Trail width:** 4 - 6 ft **Trail condition:** smooth with occasional bumps	**Location:** Wheat Ridge **Distance from downtown:** 9 mi **Drive time:** 15 min **Access:** free **Trailhead picnic tables:** yes **Trailhead restrooms:** yes **Trailhead water:** yes **Playground:** yes
Starting elevation: 5,570 ft **Elevation gain:** 60 ft	**Stroller type:** all types

Crown Hill Park is an oasis in the middle of busy Denver and is intentionally kept in a natural state with minimal development. The park has beautiful views of the Front Range, two lakes, a wildlife sanctuary for migratory birds, and a network of paved and unpaved trails. This route strings together both the outer and inner horse trails for a 3.3 mile outing that avoids most of the paved paths. The smooth, consistent gravel trail is open to all users, but remember to yield to horses should you encounter them. There is room for shortcuts and for extensions – you can easily create your own favorite route in this park. Note that the wildlife sanctuary is closed March 1 - June 30, along with its trails, boardwalk, and access to Kestrel Pond. This route starts and ends at Paramount Park, an adjacent neighborhood park with a playground and other facilities.

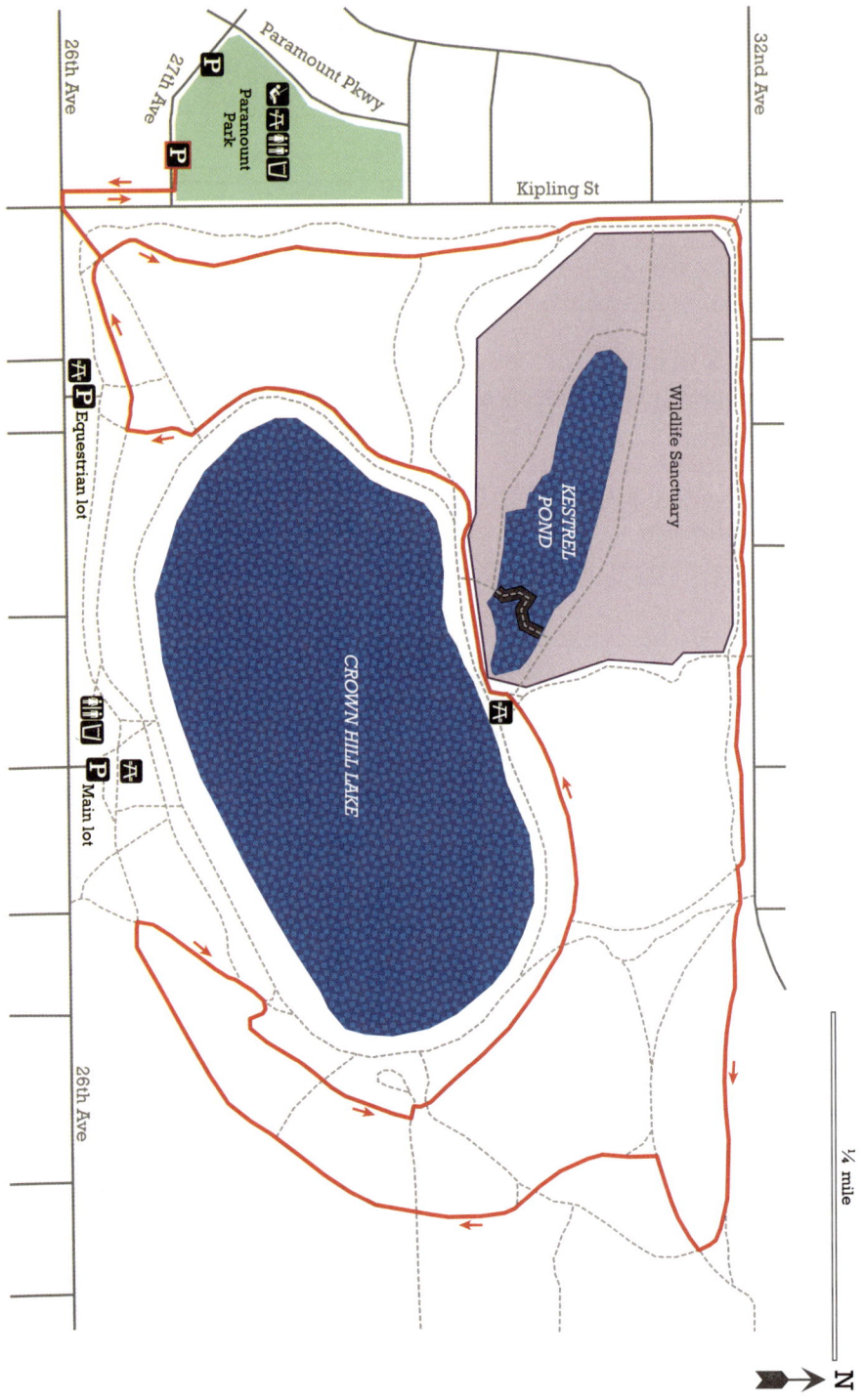

26th Ave

27th Ave

Paramount Pkwy

P

P

Paramount
Park

Kipling St

32nd Ave

Equestrian lot
P

Wildlife Sanctuary

KESTREL
POND

CROWN HILL LAKE

Main lot
P

26th Ave

N

¼ mile

Directions

From downtown Denver, drive south on I-25 and exit at West 6th Ave (exit 209B). Drive west on Hwy 6, exit at Kipling St North, and turn right. After 2.2 miles and just past 26th Ave, turn left onto 27th Ave. Immediately after the turn, park on your right, next to the baseball diamond (*10001 W 27th Ave* in Wheat Ridge). If you want to skip the playground at Paramount Park, you can leave your car in the Crown Hill Park main lot or in the smaller equestrian lot to the west.

Trail Description

Leave Paramount Park and proceed toward the intersection of Kipling St and 26th Ave (the road shoulder is paved but there is no real sidewalk; you will need to cut through a gas station). Cross the street at the crosswalk and enter Crown Hill Park on the paved path. Find the gravel trail about 150 ft past the entrance sign and turn left onto it. For the first mile, the horse trail stays close to the paved path as it circles around the park. After the outer loop, the inner loop takes you close to Crown Hill Lake before returning to the entrance. The route is not the easiest to follow since none of the trail junctions is marked with signs. But don't worry, if you miss a turn

you can always find a connecting trail to bring you back to the route described here. Have some fun and explore!

History & Info

The Crown Hill Park area was used as farmland for a century; the general lack of ecological diversity in the park speaks of its agricultural past. In 1972, when the area was rapidly being developed, a group of citizens proposed to preserve the scenic and open lands within Jefferson County. In 1978, Lakewood and Wheat Ridge joined Jefferson County in purchasing 168 acres of land, creating Crown Hill Open Space Park. The northwest corner of the park was designated a national wildlife refuge in 1991. The two bodies of water on the park property were originally natural ponds, but Crown Hill Lake was enlarged several times. Water stored in Crown Hill Lake originates in Clear Creek and is transported to the lake via a ditch. About 85% of the park's vegetation is grasslands; the remaining 15% are wetlands or riparian areas.

Special considerations

The park is open one hour before sunrise to one hour after sunset. Dogs must be on a leash. No boating, swimming, or wading. There is little consistent shade, so come prepared for full sun exposure. This is a busy park - try visiting earlier or later in the day. The wildlife sanctuary is open to hikers July 1 - Feb 28 and remains closed during the rest of the year for the protection of nesting waterfowl.

M9 DENVER METRO

Quincy Reservoir
Foot Path Gravel Loop

Length: 4.8 / 3.1 mi roundtrip **Steepness:** ◢◢(◢) 2 / 3 of 5 **Bumpy factor:** ●● 2 of 5 **Trail surface:** gravel path, paved sidewalk for 3.1 mi option **Trail width:** 4 - 7 ft **Trail condition:** smooth with some bumps, ripples, and loose gravel	**Location:** Aurora **Distance from downtown:** 19 mi **Drive time:** 25 min **Access:** $7 per adult
	Trailhead picnic tables: yes **Trailhead restrooms:** yes **Trailhead water:** no **Playground:** no
Starting elevation: 5,730 ft **Elevation gain:** 60 / 100 ft	**Stroller type:** all types, but off-road tires will do better

Quincy Reservoir is a quiet little 160 acre lake in the heart of Aurora, known for its good fishing, boating, and hiking. It offers a beautiful lake atmosphere, whether you visit in the spring or fall (shade is limited, so avoid hot summer days; the park is closed in the winter). The unpaved gravel trail circles around the reservoir but does not connect in a full loop. Two solutions are offered here: you can run around the lake, then turn and come back the same way for a nice 4.8 mile route. Or, you can proceed to the West Parking Lot and close the loop by descending to street level and using the sidewalk for your uphill return trip to the East Parking Lot (3.1 miles). There is a nice fishing dock near the East Lot and a dog park at the West Lot.

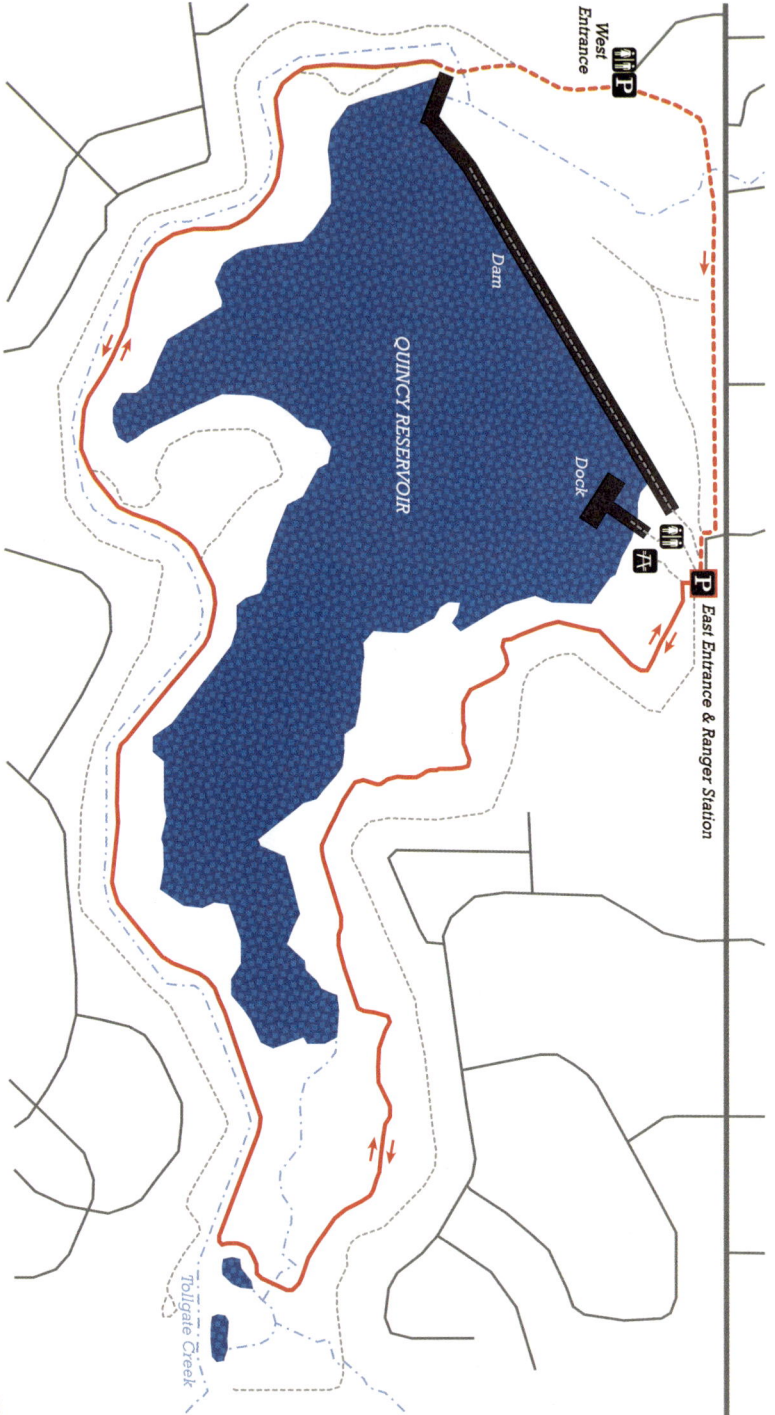

QUINCY RESERVOIR

Dam

Dock

West
Entrance

East Entrance & Ranger Station

Tollgate Creek

¼ mile

N

Directions

Take I-25 South to I-225 (exit 200). Take I-225 North to Parker Road (exit 4). Turn right and follow Parker Road south for 1.8 miles to Quincy Ave. Turn left and drive on Quincy Ave for 2.8 miles. The East Parking Lot entrance will be on your right across from the elementary school as you ascend a hill (*18350 E. Quincy Ave*). Obtain a day pass at the self-service box or at the ranger station.

Trail Description

Find the gravel trail on your left as you leave the parking lot and begin your loop trip around the lake. You will follow the tree-lined shoreline on a wavy gravel road with several ups and downs. There is a very brief paved section near the half-way point around the reservoir. Continue next to a canal (the diverted Tollgate Creek) on largely flat terrain. After a few hills you approach the dam and its spillway. Here, the trail dips steeply for 60 feet toward a foot bridge over the canal. If you are running the 4.8 mile out-and-back route, this is your turnaround point. If you choose to continue, cross the bridge and follow the access road to the West Parking Lot. Leave the lot on a dirt trail and descend to street level. Run uphill on the sidewalk along Quincy Ave for ¼ of a mile and re-enter the East Parking Lot.

History & Info

The reservoir is located on the stream bed of Tollgate Creek, but the creek itself is diverted around the lake in a canal. The majority of water in Quincy Reservoir arrives by pipeline from Rampart Reservoir in Aurora. The 38-foot tall dam was completed in 1976. The East Parking area features picnic tables, a boat launch, boat rentals, and a fishing dock.

Special considerations

Pets are prohibited at Quincy Reservoir. The park opens on March 1 and closes on October 31. Park hours are 6:00 AM - 8:30 PM in the spring and fall, 5:30 AM - 9:30 PM in the summer.

Length: 4.5 mi roundtrip	**Location:** Littleton
Steepness: ◢◢◢ 3 of 5	**Distance from downtown:** 12 mi
Bumpy factor: ✴ 1 of 5	**Drive time:** 20 min
Trail surface: dirt & gravel road; brief paved sections	**Access:** free
Trail width: 6 - 10 ft	**Trailhead picnic tables:** yes
Trail condition: smooth	**Trailhead restrooms:** yes
	Trailhead water: yes
	Playground: yes
Starting elevation: 5,500 ft	
Elevation gain: 140 ft	**Stroller type:** all types

This trail follows beautiful, tree-lined Big Dry Creek as it winds through urban and open space in Arapahoe County (the trail is not to be confused with the unrelated Big Dry Creek Trail in Westminster, route M7). Large, majestic cottonwoods alternate with grassy fields and suburban parks. While most of this smooth trail is flat or at a very gentle grade, a few sections may cause you to stop and walk your stroller. The tall trees provide cool shade in the summer and create visual interest in the winter. Three playgrounds are scattered along this route, so plan on a few playtime breaks with the kids.

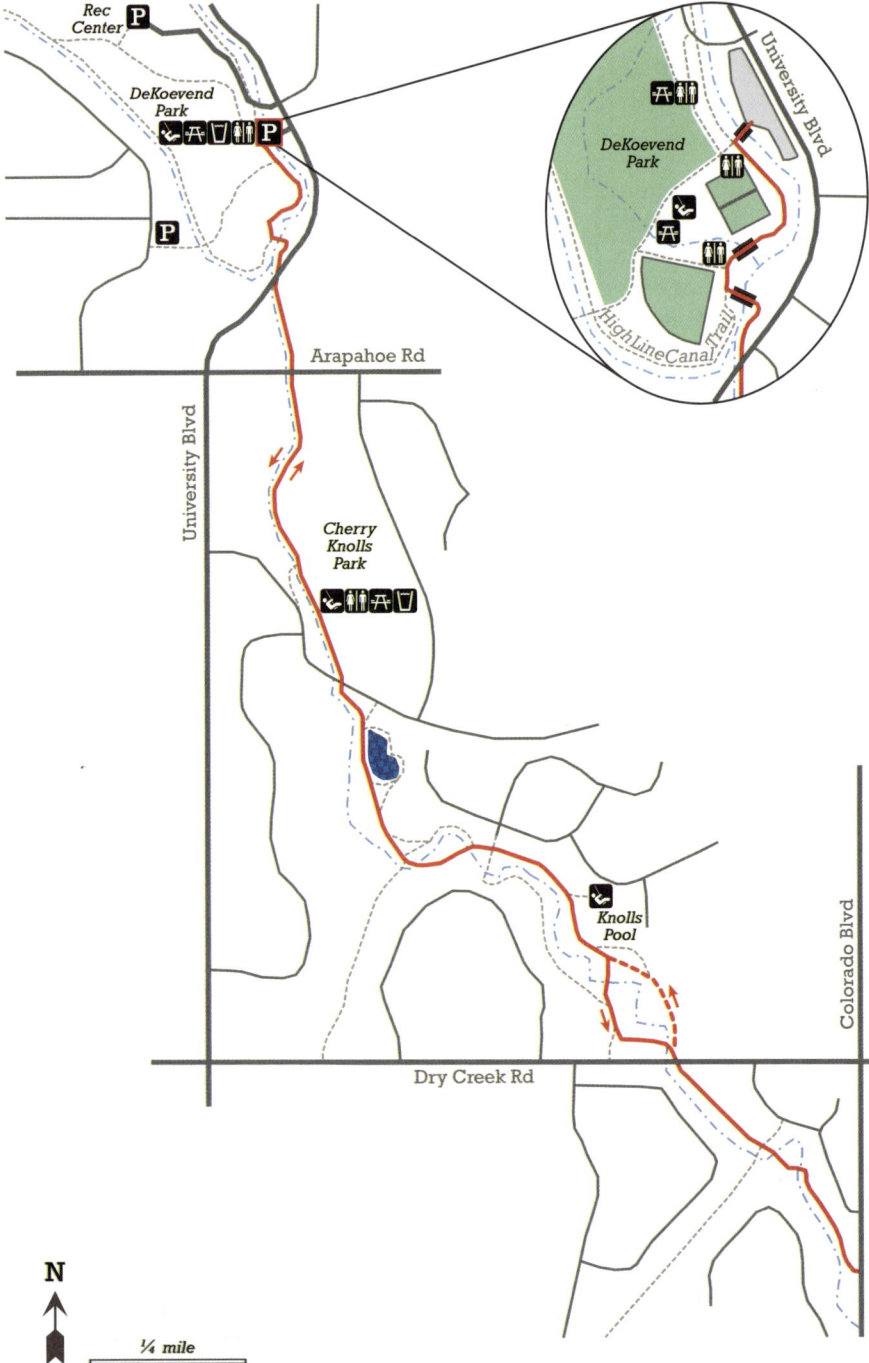

Rec
Center

DeKoevend
Park

DeKoevend
Park

University Blvd

High Line Canal Trail

Arapahoe Rd

University Blvd

Cherry
Knolls
Park

Knolls
Pool

Colorado Blvd

Dry Creek Rd

N

¼ mile

Directions

Drive south on I-25 and exit at University Blvd (exit 205). Turn right and follow University Blvd south for about 6 miles. Immediately after the turnoff to the Goodson Rec Center, turn right into the parking lot for Julia DeKoevend Park. There are two alternative parking options if the park lot is full: the Goodson Rec Center to the north and the South Suburban Ice Arena to the west.

Trail Description

Following this wide trail is easy; the only tricky part is locating its start point. Out of the parking lot on University Blvd, cross the narrow pedestrian bridge over the High Line Canal. Turn left onto the High Line Canal Trail and follow it for 800 feet, past tennis courts, over another bridge, and past a baseball field. As the trail turns left and you go uphill, look for a bridge on your left with a Trail System map next to it.

This marks the beginning of the Big Dry Creek Trail. Cross this bridge and follow the trail through several underpasses. During the next 2 miles you will run gently uphill on a smooth, wide dirt road with several brief steep uphill segments. Side trails branch off along the main route but these are mostly singletrack detours. Expansive Cherry Knolls Park beckons for a playground stop, and a third playground can be found off the main road (near the Knolls Pool) two-thirds of the way to the turn-around point. Shortly after that, take a right at the fork in the road for a brief downhill section. The trail ends at Colorado Blvd, near the South Suburban Golf Course. On your way back, you may take a right at the fork for an optional short uphill detour above the creek.

History & Info

The Big Dry Creek Trail has two segments: the unpaved southeast section featured here and a paved northwest section (completed in 2009). The two segments are connected by a 2-mile portion of the High Line Canal Trail.

Special considerations

Cherry Knolls Park features a wildlife-themed playground for small kids. Just south of Cherry Knolls, there is a play area built in the creek itself, widened and paved with flat stones in the water. DeKoevend Park at the trailhead has a large playground and also provides picnic shelters, a lighted baseball field, a multi-purpose field, tennis courts, and a basketball court.

South Suburban Trails
Lee Gulch Trail

Length: 4.0 / 4.6 mi roundtrip **Steepness:** ◢◢◢ 3 of 5 **Bumpy factor:** ❄ 1 of 5 **Trail surface:** dirt & gravel road **Trail width:** 6 - 10 ft **Trail condition:** smooth	**Location:** Littleton **Distance from downtown:** 12 mi **Drive time:** 25 min **Access:** free
	Trailhead picnic tables: yes **Trailhead restrooms:** no **Trailhead water:** yes **Playground:** yes
Starting elevation: 5,380 ft **Elevation gain:** 150 / 200 ft	**Stroller type:** all types

The 4.4-mile long Lee Gulch Trail connects the Platte River Trail to the High Line Canal Trail in Littleton. It contains paved and soft surface sections and follows Lee Gulch as it makes its way to the South Platte River. The nice 2-mile segment featured here is unpaved and begins at Charley Emley Park, a small neighborhood park with a playground. The tranquil trail leads uphill along the gulch, passing through grassy parkland, by a small pond, and through several meadows. There are some ups and downs in this out-and-back route but no seriously steep sections (the exception is in the optional extension at the end). In the summer, the abundant trees and bushes nicely camouflage the many houses lining the trail; in the winter its suburban setting becomes more obvious.

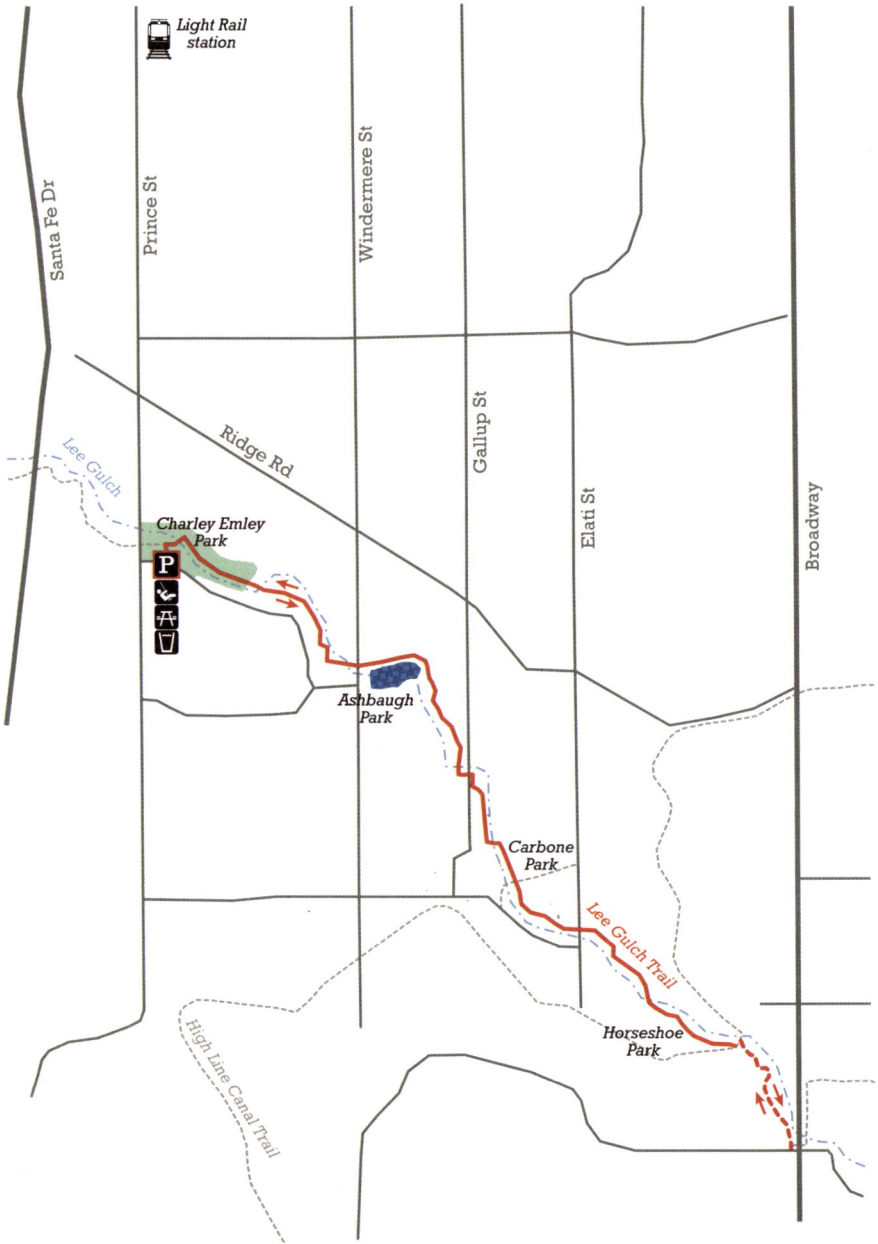

Light Rail station

Santa Fe Dr

Prince St

Windermere St

Gallup St

Elati St

Broadway

Ridge Rd

Lee Gulch

Charley Emley Park

P

Ashbaugh Park

Carbone Park

Lee Gulch Trail

Horseshoe Park

High Line Canal Trail

N

¼ mile

Directions

Drive south on I-25 and take exit 207B. Drive south on Santa Fe Drive for about 7 miles. Just past downtown Littleton, turn left onto Church Ave. Turn right onto Prince St and drive south for 1 mile, then turn left onto Briarwood Ave. Charley Emley Park is on your left (*2332 W Briarwood Ave*); ample street parking is available on Briarwood Ave. Note that some maps incorrectly label this location as Lower Ridgewood Park. The trailhead is located about 1.2 miles from the Littleton/Downtown light rail station (C/D line).

Trail Description

Follow the short paved path down the hill past the playground and cross a bridge. Turn right and you will be on the unpaved Lee Gulch Trail. The wide path is generally easy to follow; there are several (paved) side trails. You will cross over many bridges, pass through parks, and run through densely vegetated areas. At times, the trail runs at the bottom of the Lee Gulch canyon, other sections take you across wide meadows higher up. Houses encroach on the green space but for the most part tower above the trail. When you reach the intersection with the High Line Canal Trail, either turn around or continue along the optional route extension to Broadway. This will add 0.6 miles to your trip and includes a steep ascent. Enjoy your return trip, mostly downhill, to Charley Emley Park.

History & Info

The Lee Gulch Trail is a vital link for the Southbridge neighborhood and is often used by cyclists and distance runners who wish to connect the High Line, Platte River, and Big Dry Creek trails in a 15-mile loop.

Special considerations

Charley Emley Park also features tennis courts, a basketball court, and a picnic shelter. Swimming or wading are not permitted in the pond at Ashbaugh Park. The trail is open daily from 6:00 AM to 11:00 PM. Pets must be on a leash.

Coal Creek Regional Trail
Louisville section

Length: 5.4 / 6.3 mi roundtrip **Steepness:** ▲▲▲ 3 of 5 **Bumpy factor:** ✸ 1 of 5 **Trail surface:** dirt & gravel road; several short paved sections **Trail width:** 6 - 10 ft **Trail condition:** smooth	**Location:** Louisville **Distance from downtown:** 20 mi **Drive time:** 30 min **Access:** free
	Trailhead picnic tables: yes **Trailhead restrooms:** yes **Trailhead water:** yes **Playground:** yes
Starting elevation: 5,330 ft **Elevation gain:** 260 / 320 ft	**Stroller type:** all types

The Coal Creek Trail is the product of a joint effort between Louisville, Lafayette, Superior, Broomfield, Erie, and Boulder Counties. The segment featured here runs

along the creek in the southern part of Louisville. It begins and ends at Louisville Community Park, a nice park with ponds, a playground, picnic shelters, a dog park, and a mini spray-ground. The trail starts out deceptively flat, but has one significant hill toward the end of the first mile, earning this route the higher steepness rating. As long as you resign yourself to walking your stroller in this brief section, you will enjoy the beautiful 5.4 mile out-and-back run in a scenic setting. The final stretch is optional for a roundtrip total of 6.3 miles. Alternatively, if you want to skip the hill altogether (along with the playground), you can park at the Public Road turn-around point and explore the trail east-to-west from there (about 4 miles roundtrip).

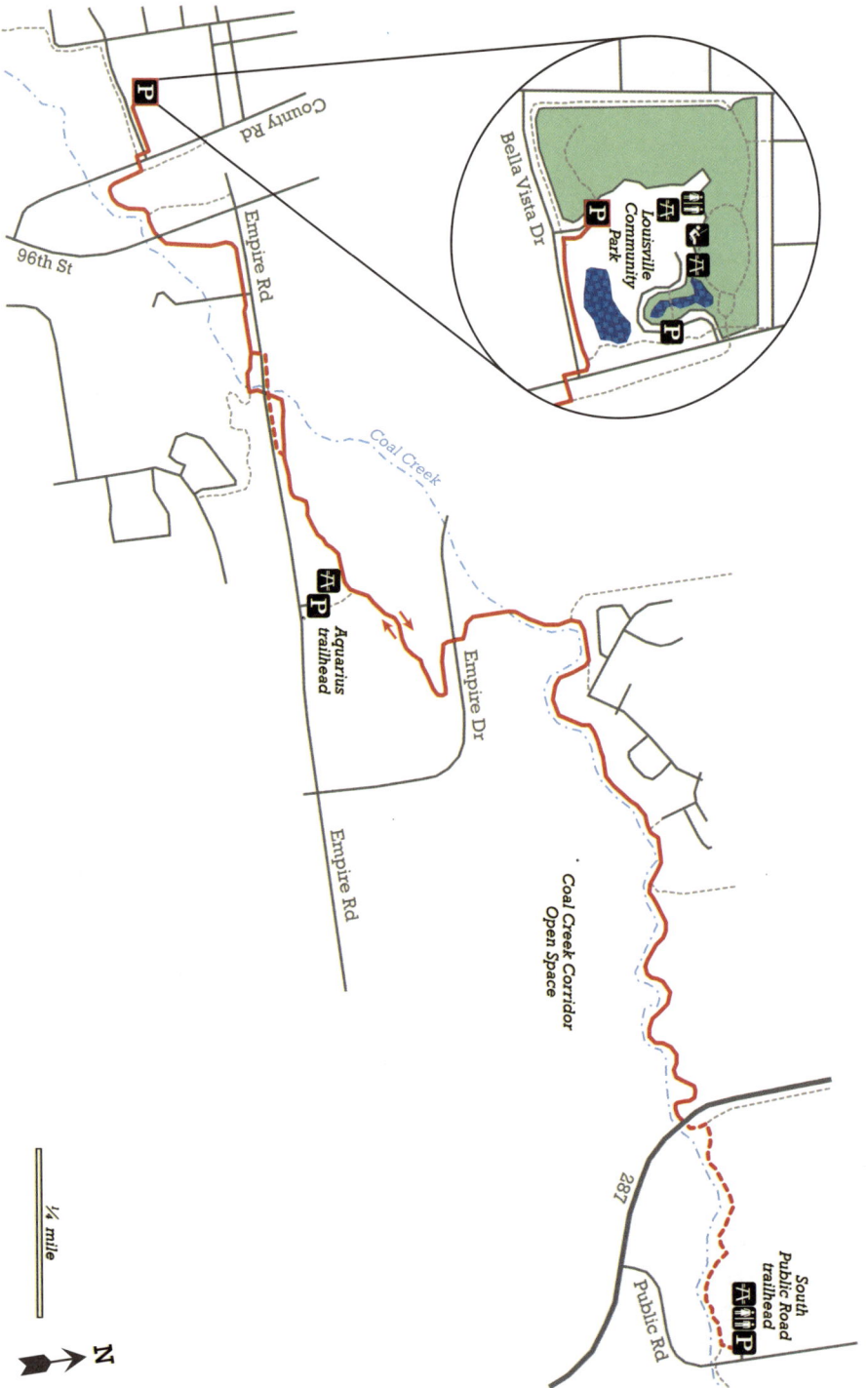

County Rd

96th St

Empire Rd

Bella Vista Dr

Louisville
Community
Park

Coal Creek

Aquarius
trailhead

Empire Dr

Empire Rd

Coal Creek Corridor
Open Space

287

Public Rd

South
Public Road
trailhead

¼ mile

N

Directions

Drive north on I-25 and take exit 217A to US-36 toward Boulder. Go west on highway 36 and exit at StorageTek Drive. Turn right onto 96th St/StorageTek Dr. Just before the entrance to the Northwest Parkway toll road, turn left onto 96th St. After 1.3 miles, turn left onto County Rd. After 0.3 miles, turn left onto Bella Vista Dr. Louisville Community Park will be on your right; follow the road to the south parking lot (*955 Bella Vista Dr*).

Trail Description

Follow the sidewalk on Bella Vista Drive to County Road. Cross both streets, then head east (right) on the Coal Creek Trail. After the underpasses below the railroad tracks and 96th St, the trail parallels Empire Rd and then crosses underneath it. In the spring, this underpass is often flooded. If this occurs, backtrack 500 feet to a short spur trail leading up to Empire Road (see map); cross the road and run along its wide shoulder for about 800 feet; rejoin the Coal Creek Trail on the northern side of the road, just below the shoulder. After first ascending and then descending the steep grassland hill, the trail follows Coal Creek Trail more closely for

the remainder of the route. This portion is shaded by large trees and you are never too far from the creek. Beware of several side trails branching off Coal Creek Trail (often these side trails are as wide as the main trail). Turn around when you reach the Hwy 287 underpass, or make a sharp right turn and proceed along Coal Creek to the Public Road parking lot about half a mile further down the trail.

History & Info

The creek's name derives from the highly productive coal fields found in this area. The town of Louisville itself dates back to the opening of the first coal mine in 1877

(the last coal mines operating in Louisville closed in the 1950s). The central portion of the Coal Creek Regional Trail was constructed and opened in the early 1990s. Louisville Community Park opened in 2006.

Special considerations

Pedestrians, bicyclists, and dogs are allowed on the trail. Equestrians are not permitted due to Louisville city regulations. Pets must be on a leash and under control at all times. Unauthorized motor vehicles are prohibited.

74

Standley Lake Regional Park
Big Dry Creek / Dam Trail

Length: 3.4 / 4.0 mi roundtrip **Steepness:** ◣◣◣◣◣ 5 of 5 **Bumpy factor:** ●● 2 of 5 **Trail surface:** crushed gravel and dirt road **Trail width:** 6 - 10 ft **Trail condition:** largely smooth with occasional ruts	**Location:** Westminster **Distance from downtown:** 16 mi **Drive time:** 25 min **Access:** free
	Trailhead picnic tables: nearby **Trailhead restrooms:** nearby **Trailhead water:** nearby **Playground:** no
Starting elevation: 5,540 ft **Elevation gain:** 260 / 280 ft	**Stroller type:** double strollers not encouraged due to steepness

This suburban route begins with a downhill section and continues in an up-and-down fashion through rolling terrain. Our kids call this the "stroller coaster" trail and you will understand why after you run it; the elevation change will have you huffing and puffing. The route makes a nice hike or a challenging workout run. Plants and animals common to this area include native grasses, wildflowers, cottonwoods, prairie dogs, hawks, and meadowlarks. There are few trees along this trail and the area is often extremely windy (avoid it on blustery days). The optional loop near the end is nearly flat but can be muddy after rains or snow melt. Restrooms and picnic tables are available at the nearby Regional Park campground.

N

¼ mile

100th Ave

entrance station

camp ground

STANDLEY LAKE

86th Pkwy

P

Dam

P

Big Dry Creek Trail

LOON LAKE

Big Dry Creek Trail

88th Ave

P

100th Ave

Directions

Take I-25 North to highway 36 toward Boulder. Go west on highway 36 and exit at Church Ranch Blvd. Turn left, cross the highway and continue on Church Ranch Blvd. At the intersection with Wadsworth Pkwy, continue straight. After 1.5 miles, turn left at Owen Street. Park in the free trailhead parking lot located at 100th Ave and Owens St in Westminster.

Trail Description

Enter the Big Dry Creek Trail through an opening in the wooden fence just wide enough for a double stroller. Go east (left) on the wide gravel trail. It gradually descends next to the Standley Lake spillway with its many amphitheater-like concrete steps (designed to slow down water and thereby prevent erosion). Pass by Loon Lake on your left and continue for another 1,000 ft. Then leave the Big Dry Creek Trail by turning right onto a steeply descending trail (this is the steepest section of the route). Cross the spillway and ascend on the other side. You are now running parallel to the dam. Keep going up - you will be rewarded with nice views of Standley Lake at the top. At 1.7 miles you reach an abandoned dirt parking lot on

your right, next to the shoreline. For the optional 0.6 mile extension, proceed south on the dirt road leading out of the lot and loop back on a wide double track back to the dirt lot. This loop is quite picturesque (with great views of the lake) and well worth the detour. Then retrace the stroller coaster route back to your car.

History & Info

Standley Lake Dam was constructed between 1909 and 1919; it was enlarged in 1963. At capacity, the lake is 96 feet deep at the face of the dam. The water from the reservoir is used as a municipal water supply for the cities of Westminster, Northglenn and Thornton. The City of Westminster began managing the area as a lake park in 1970; the area was designated a Regional Park in 1998.

Special considerations

Park hours are 7:30 AM to sunset. The trailhead parking lot has gates that are locked sunset-to-sunrise. Please stay off the mile-long Standley Lake dam. No swimming or wading is allowed in the reservoir. All pets must be on a leash. The west portion of Standley Lake Regional Park offers a marina, campground, boat ramp, visitor center, and other facilities (but access by car requires a fee at the entrance station).

M14 Cherry Creek State Park - Cottonwood Creek Trail

Length: 3.8 mi. **Steepness**: 2 of 5. **Bumpy factor**: 1 of 5. **Trail surface**: gravel path. **Trail width**: 6-9 ft. **Trail condition**: smooth. **Starting elevation**: 5,560 ft. **Elevation gain**: 60 ft. **Location**: Aurora. **Distance from downtown**: 15 mi. **Drive time**: 25 min. **Access**: $9 per car. **Trailhead picnic tables**: no. **Trailhead restrooms**: yes. **Trailhead water**: no. **Playground**: no. **Stroller type**: all types.

This out-and-back route is located in the state park's open grassland. Start at the Cottonwood Creek trailhead, about 2 miles from the West Entrance. The trail loosely follows Cottonwood Creek on a gentle uphill slope, crossing the creek several times. Go as far as you like or proceed all the way to the Peoria Street underpass for a 3.8 mile roundtrip run. Despite its name, you won't find too many trees along this trail; it is primarily prairie-riparian habitat. See route M3 for directions and history information for the state park.

M15 Coyote Run Open Space - Harper Lake / Coyote Run

Length: 3.2 mi. **Steepness**: 3 of 5. **Bumpy factor**: 1 of 5. **Trail surface**: dirt road & gravel path. **Trail width**: 5-8 ft. **Trail condition**: mostly smooth. **Starting elevation**: 5,610 ft. **Elevation gain**: 150 ft. **Location**: Louisville. **Distance from downtown**: 21 mi. **Drive time**: 25 min. **Access**: free. **Trailhead picnic tables**: no. **Trailhead restrooms**: yes. **Trailhead water**: no. **Playground**: no. **Stroller type**: all types.

Here is a lovely suburban Open Space route with some considerable hills. Park at the Leon A Wurl Wildlife Sanctuary parking lot. Begin in a counter-clockwise direction along the Harper Lake loop trail, then take the connector trail to Coyote Run Open Space. Proceed until the gravel path turns into a paved path; turn around when you reach either Boulder Rd or Via Appia Way. On your return, complete the loop around Harper Lake and return to the parking lot. About half-way around the lake, a short side trail to a playground beckons (*929 W Alder St*). The Wildlife Sanctuary parking lot is located on the corner of McCaslin Blvd and Washington Ave in Louisville.

M16 Colorado Hills Open Space - Westminster Hills Trail

Length: 2.3 / 4.2 mi. **Steepness**: 3 of 5. **Bumpy factor**: 3 of 5. **Trail surface**: dirt & rocks. **Trail width**: 3-10 ft. **Trail condition**: rocky in parts; ruts and boulders. **Starting elevation**: 5,515 ft. **Elevation gain**: 150 / 260 ft. **Location**: Westminster. **Distance from downtown**: 17 mi. **Drive time:** 25 min. **Access:** free. **Trailhead picnic tables**: no. **Trailhead restrooms**: no. **Trailhead water**: no. **Playground**: no. **Stroller type**: off-road recommended.

Most people come here to visit the large off-leash dog park, but once you ascend on the trail past the irrigation ditch you will quickly find solitude. You can run or walk the 2.3-mile loop or pass through a gate in the middle of the loop and add on an out-and-back visit to the little pond at trail's end (Mower Reservoir) for a 4.2 mile total route. The trail is wide but quite bumpy with lots of loose rocks; the trail past the gate is double track. There is no shade here; this is prairie terrain. Look for great views of the Front Range mountains, foothills, and surrounding plains. Prairie dog holes are everywhere; the pond has seasonal water only. The trailhead is located at 105th Avenue and Simms Street in Westminster.

M17 Bluffs Regional Park - Loop trail

Length: 2.7 mi. **Steepness**: 5 of 5. **Bumpy factor**: 2 of 5. **Trail surface**: gravel & dirt road. **Trail width**: 6-8 ft. **Trail condition**: largely smooth with occasional ruts. **Starting elevation**: 6,050 ft. **Elevation gain**: 380 ft. **Location**: Lone Tree. **Distance from downtown**: 20 mi. **Drive time:** 25 min. **Access:** free. **Trailhead picnic tables**: yes. **Trailhead restrooms**: yes. **Trailhead water**: no. **Playground**: nearby. **Stroller type**: double strollers not encouraged due to steepness.

This short but challenging workout takes you on an up-and-down route on a wide trail in a scenic urban setting. You are rewarded by panoramic views of the Front Range and of downtown Denver. Since there is no shade, avoid this route on hot days. The loop is best run in a counterclockwise direction, saving the final 200-foot descent for last. There are swings below the parking lot; you can find a large playground at Prairie Sky Park nearby. There also is a playground near the half-way point of the loop, less than ¼ mile from the trail (use the Dacre Connector trail). The main trailhead is located on Crooked Stick Trail in Lone Tree.

Jeff Co Open Space
Fairmount Trail

Length: 5.5 mi roundtrip **Steepness:** ◣◣ 2 of 5 **Bumpy factor:** ●● 2 of 5 **Trail surface:** dirt & gravel road; paved path **Trail width:** 2 - 6 ft **Trail condition:** some ruts and rocks	**Location:** Golden **Distance from downtown:** 18 mi **Drive time:** 30 min **Access:** free **Trailhead picnic tables:** yes **Trailhead restrooms:** no **Trailhead water:** no **Playground:** yes
Starting elevation: 5,820 ft **Elevation gain:** 110 ft	**Stroller type:** double strollers not encouraged due to trail width

Jefferson County's Fairmount Trail bridges the cities of Arvada and Golden, cutting through residential and rural Open Space lands. It closely follows the Boulder Diversion Canal on its way south to Clear Creek. This route starts at Apple Meadows Park, a quiet neighborhood park with a playground and picnic tables, and connects to the Fairmount Trail via a short paved trail segment. There is little shade along the Fairmount Trail, so avoid the middle of the day. Nice views of the foothills and North Table Mountain are plentiful along the route. The grade is gentle, with a few ups and downs along the way. Note that most of the trail is a wide dirt road but some parts look more like a double track path, so double strollers are not recommended here.

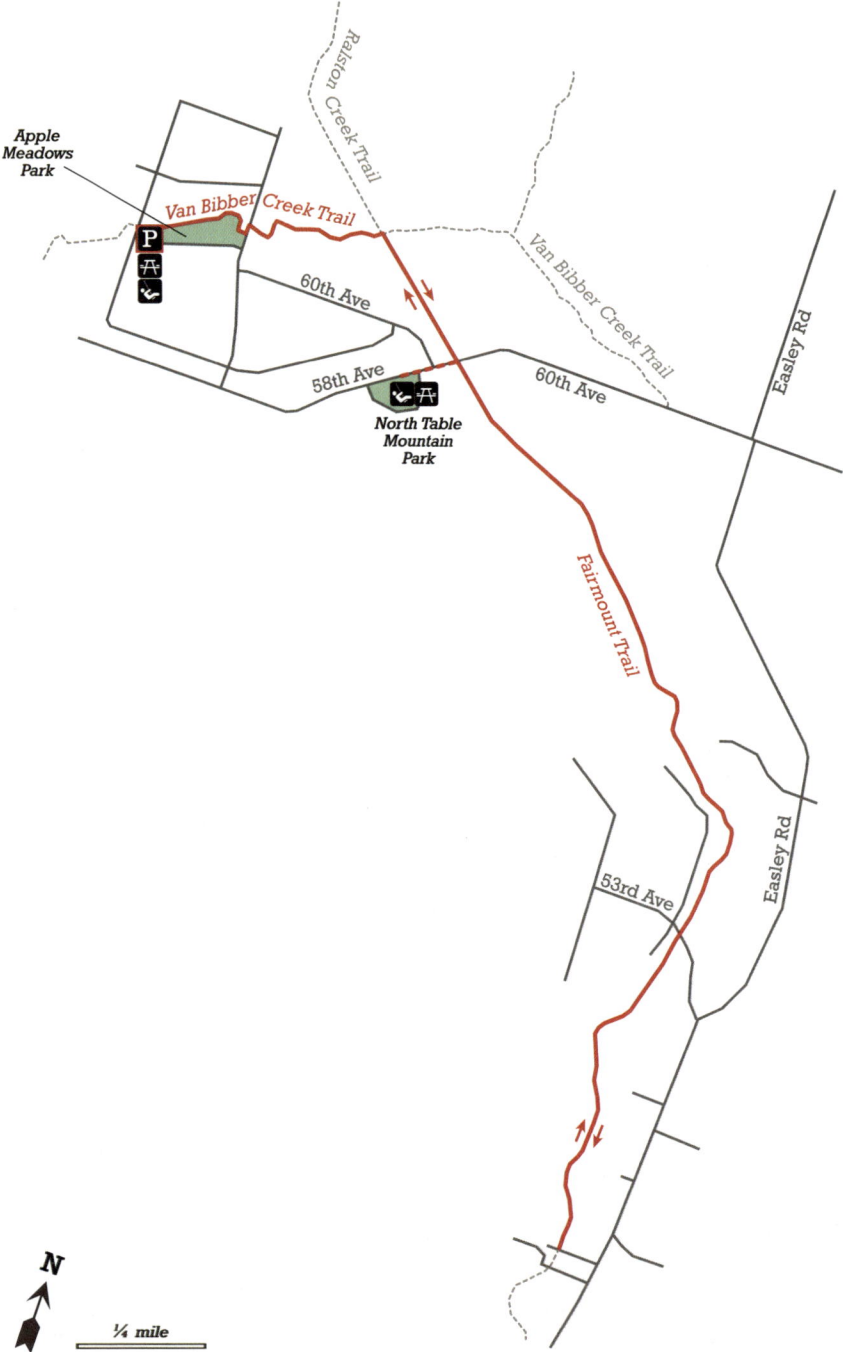

Apple
Meadows
Park

Van Bibber Creek Trail

Ralston Creek Trail

Van Bibber Creek Trail

Easley Rd

60th Ave

58th Ave

North Table
Mountain
Park

60th Ave

Fairmount Trail

Easley Rd

53rd Ave

N

¼ mile

Directions

Drive west on I-70 to exit 265. Merge onto Hwy 58 west toward Golden. After 1.5 miles, take the McIntyre St exit and turn right. Drive north for 2.2 miles. Turn left onto 60th Ave and drive west for 1.7 miles. Just after crossing the Fairmount Trail, turn right to stay on 60th Ave. Turn right at Crestone St, then immediately left onto 60th Place. After 0.2 miles, Apple Meadows Park will be on your right (*19080 W 60th Pl*). An alternative starting point is the playground at North Table Mountain Park (*18300 W 58th Dr*); starting from there shortens this route to a 4.1 mile roundtrip outing.

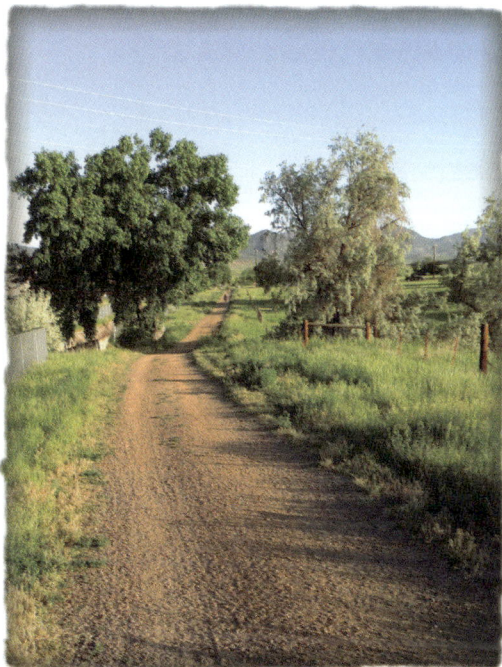

Trail Description

From Apple Meadows Park, take the paved Van Bibber Creek Trail east for about half a mile to its intersection with the unpaved Fairmount Trail. Turn right and

proceed south for 2.2 miles to the turnaround point. The trail follows the irrigation ditch, with North Table Mountain to the west as your steady companion and homes of every size and shape lining the trail. Scenic views of the mountains and the Denver skyline accompany your every step. You may also see deer along the trail. As you proceed along the path, the trail begins to resemble a double track trail; stay on the right to allow cyclists and other runners to pass. A good point to turn back is the crossing of a dirt road, about 0.7 miles after crossing paved 53rd Ave. You could venture south beyond this point, but here the trail is considerably rockier and a bit steeper.

History & Info

The Fairmount Trail is managed cooperatively by Jefferson County Open Space and Denver Water. The irrigation canal stretches from Boulder County through Golden and belongs to the Denver Water Board. It was built to carry water from Gross Reservoir to the Ralston Reservoir area and Clear Creek, replacing water downstream in the South Platte River that Denver takes out of the upper South Platte River. At its northern end, the Fairmount Trail connects to Arvada's Ralston Creek Trail.

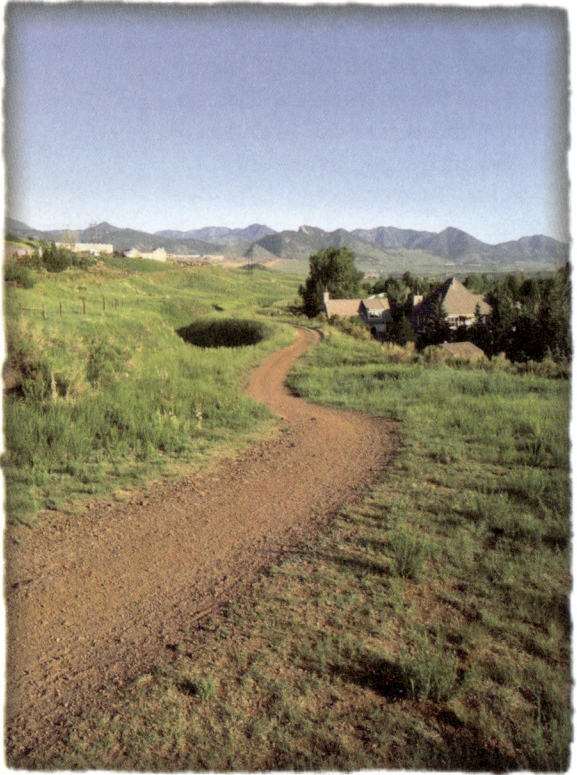

Special considerations

Dogs must be on a leash. Park hours are 1 hour before sunrise to 1 hour after sunset. Entry into the irrigation ditch is not permitted. Please respect the privacy of property owners adjacent to the trail.

L2 — LOWER FOOTHILLS

Jeff Co Open Space
Grant-Terry Trail

Length: 3.2 mi roundtrip **Steepness:** ▲▲ 2 of 5 **Bumpy factor:** ●● 2 of 5 **Trail surface:** dirt & gravel road; paved path **Trail width:** 5-15 ft **Trail condition:** smooth with a few ruts and bumps	**Location:** Golden **Distance from downtown:** 17 mi **Drive time:** 25 min **Access:** free
	Trailhead picnic tables: yes **Trailhead restrooms:** yes **Trailhead water:** yes **Playground:** yes
Starting elevation: 5,680 ft **Elevation gain:** 150 ft	**Stroller type:** all types, but off-road tires will do better

The Grant-Terry Trail is a wide unpaved path along Clear Creek in Golden. Even on hot days, the cool breeze from the creek and shade from the large trees make this a wonderful trail for a stroller hike or short run. This route starts at Lions Park near downtown Golden, featuring a large playground and other amenities. The initial portion of the route is paved but west of 6th Ave it is a soft-surface trail. The waters of Clear Creek and Church Ditch accompany the trail nearly continuously.

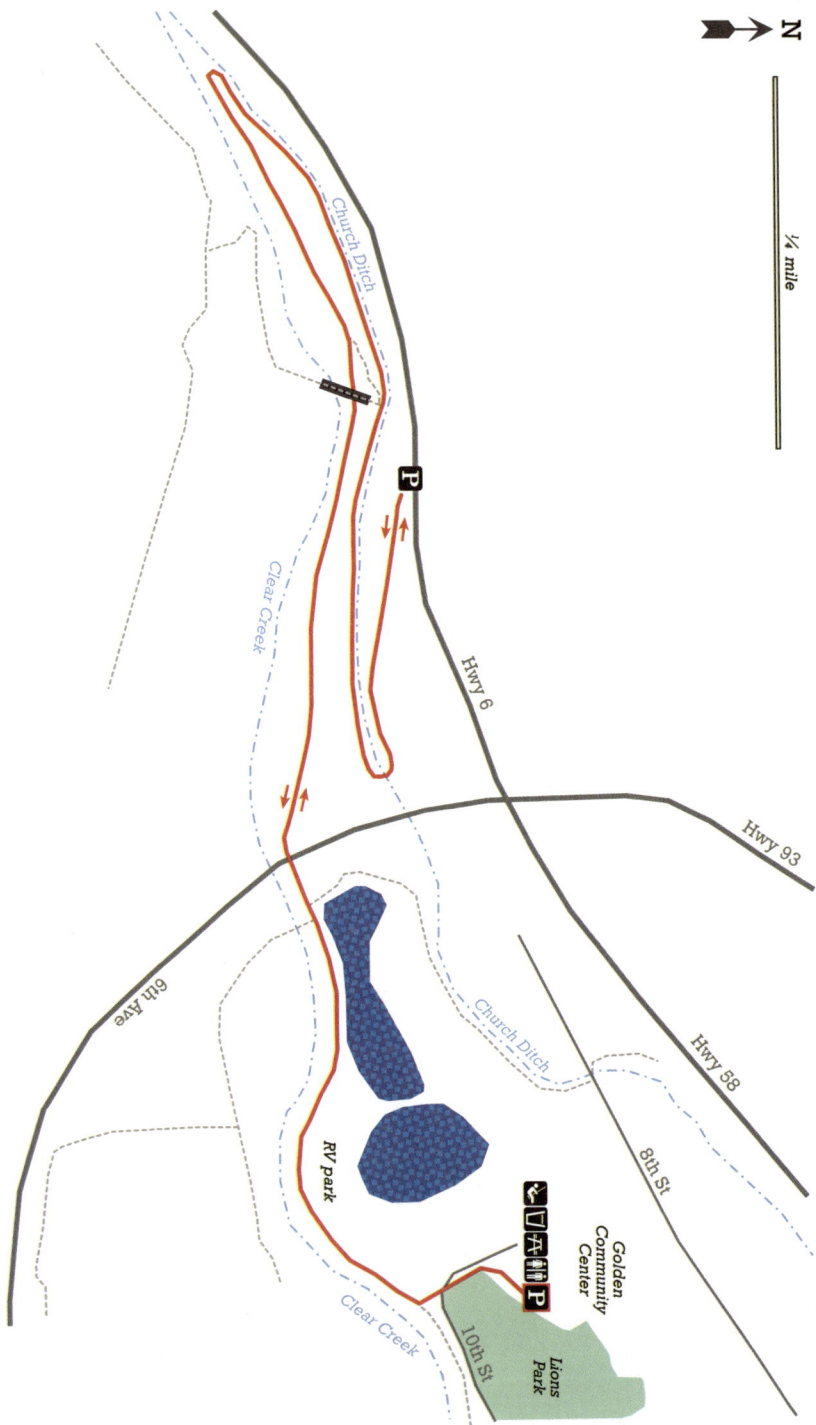

N

¼ mile

Church Ditch

Clear Creek

P

Hwy 6

Hwy 93

Hwy 58

6th Ave

Church Ditch

8th St

RV park

Clear Creek

10th St

Golden Community Center

Lions Park

Directions

Drive west on I-70 to exit 265. Merge onto Hwy 58 west toward Golden. After 4.6 miles, take the Washington Ave exit and turn left. Drive for 0.3 miles on Washington Ave, then turn right onto 10th Street. Proceed for about 0.5 miles, until 10th Street dead-ends at the Golden Community Center parking lot.

Trail Description

From Lions Park, find the paved trail running alongside Clear Creek. Proceed upstream, passing by a large RV park and two ponds. Cross under 6th Ave and continue on the wide dirt road along the creek. In the spring and summer, you might find puddles and wet spots here along the trail from water leaking out of Church Ditch above. At the first switchback turn, the headgate for Church Ditch is on your left. The trail now closely follows the ditch. Stay on the dirt trail as you pass by the bridge over the creek on your right side. After the second switchback, the path narrows and ascends to the parking lot on Hwy 6. Turn

around there and retrace your steps back to Lions Park. Be sure to explore the bridge across Clear Creek for views of the river and the canyon.

History & Info

Grant Terry Park at Clear Creek Canyon was established by Jefferson County in 1997. Church Ditch was constructed in 1906 and runs 26 miles from Golden to Westminster.

Special considerations

Dogs must be on a leash. Park hours are 1 hour before sunrise to 1 hour after sunset. It is your responsibility to know and obey Open Space rules and regulations.

L3
LOWER FOOTHILLS

Waterton Canyon
Waterton Canyon Trail

Length: 6.9 mi roundtrip
Steepness: ◢◢ 2 of 5
Bumpy factor: ●● 2 of 5
Trail surface: dirt & gravel road
Trail width: 25 ft
Trail condition: smooth with a few ruts and small rocks

Starting elevation: 5,510 ft
Elevation gain: 130 ft

Location: Littleton
Distance from downtown: 22 mi
Drive time: 35 min
Access: free

Trailhead picnic tables: yes
Trailhead restrooms: yes
Trailhead water: no
Playground: no

Stroller type: all types

Waterton Canyon is a beautiful gorge which boasts the South Platte River at its base (with plenty of fishing opportunities), herds of bighorn sheep along its walls, and a super-wide dirt trail at a gentle grade running through it. The route featured here uses the Marston Diversion Dam as a turnaround point, but you can continue up the dirt road for a roundtrip total of 12.5 miles and 330 ft elevation gain. Steepness tends to increase the further you venture into the canyon. The upper canyon walls provide some shade, but the lower areas are fully exposed to the sun. There are two neighborhood playgrounds about a mile from the trailhead.

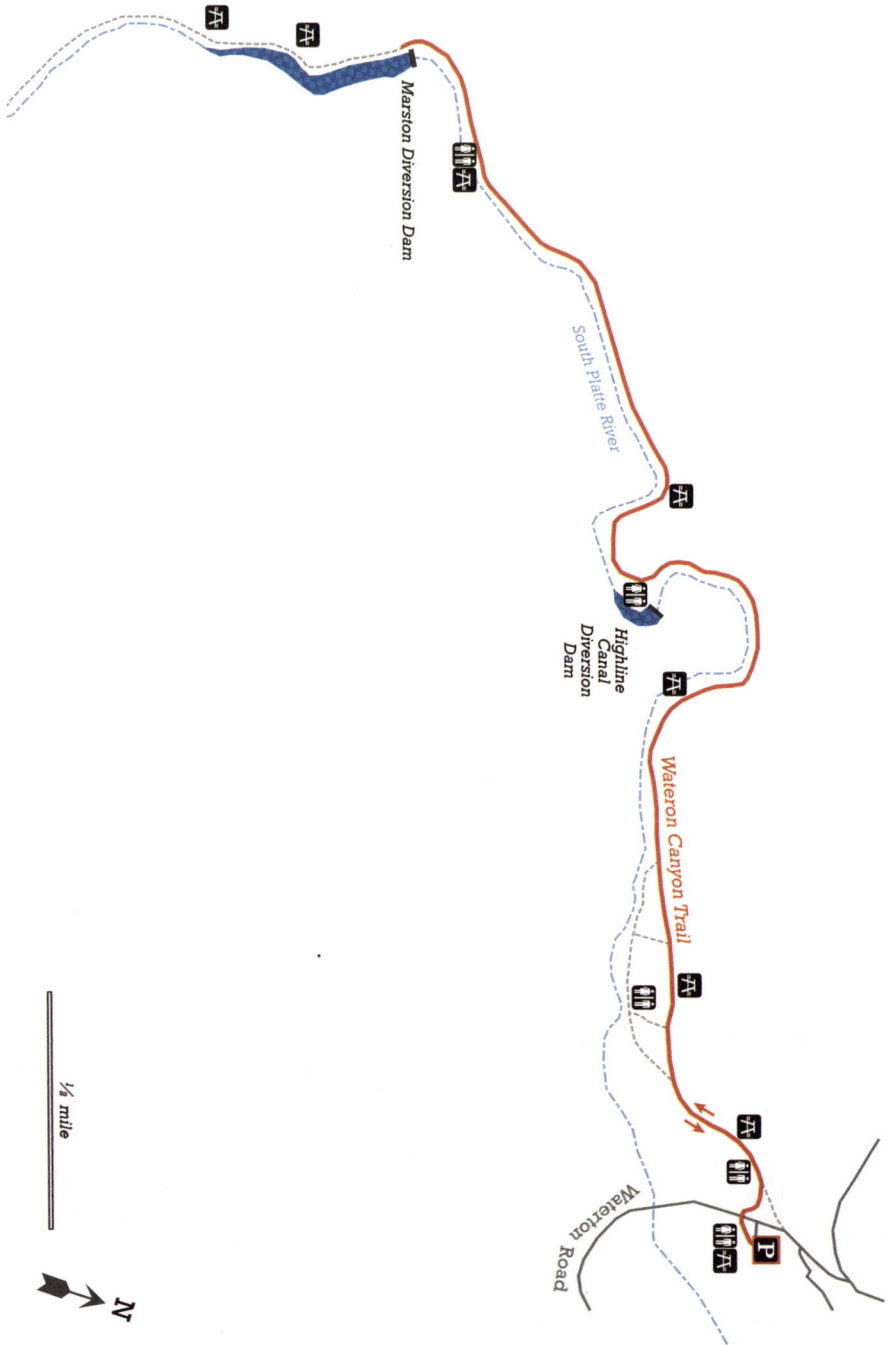

Marston Diversion Dam

South Platte River

Highline
Canal
Diversion
Dam

Wateron Canyon Trail

Waterton

Road

½ mile

N

Directions

Drive south on I-25 and take exit 207B. Drive south on Santa Fe Drive for about 9 miles and then turn right onto C-470 West. Exit at Wadsworth Blvd, turn left, and go south for 4.4 miles. Turn left onto Waterton Rd; after ¼ mile, turn left into the marked Waterton Canyon parking lot.

Trail Description

Access the trail by crossing Waterton Rd and, after a short paved section, proceed along the wide dirt road. The first mile is nearly flat and a bit industrial; after that you enter the secluded canyon and proceed uphill on a gentle grade. About halfway to the turnaround point you pass by the High Line Canal Diversion Dam and its small lake. Turn around when you reach the second diversion dam, for a 7-mile roundtrip outing. The scenic canyon makes the miles fly by, but don't hesitate to turn around before the dam. There are also numerous picnic tables and restrooms along the trail, creating some lovely picnic opportunities if you need a break. You may see bighorn sheep and mule deer in the canyon.

History & Info

The trail serves as Denver Water's maintenance road to the Strontia Springs Dam, located over six miles up Waterton Canyon. Water is diverted from the reservoir, completed in 1983, and used as drinking water for Denver. The Waterton Canyon Trail was closed from 2010 to 2012 to allow for sediment dredging operations at Strontia Springs Reservoir. In addition to bighorn sheep, the canyon also hosts more than 40 species of birds. There is a small neighborhood playground with picnic tables and a restroom about 1 mile from the trailhead (near *8563 Liverpool Circle* in Littleton), and another playground is located near *8291 Liverpool Circle.*

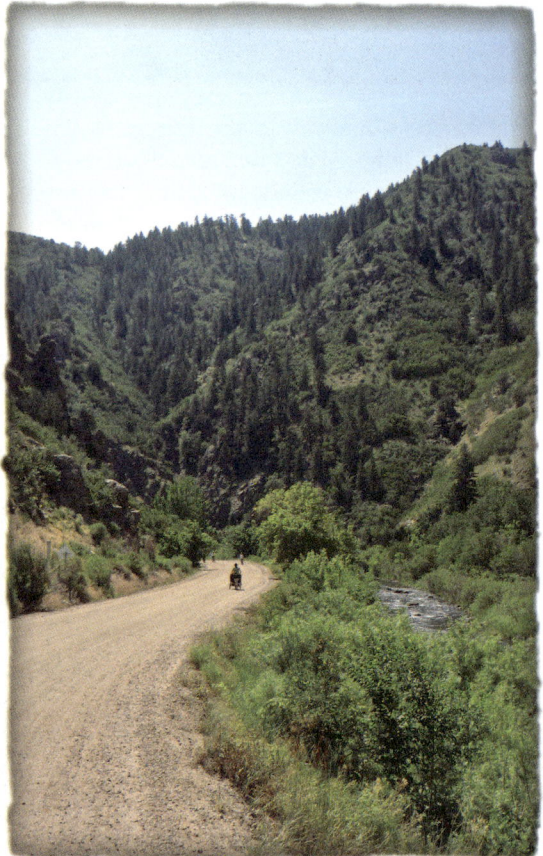

Special considerations

Dogs are not allowed in the canyon for the protection of the bighorn sheep. Swimming, wading, and boating are prohibited. Waterton Canyon is open a half hour before sunrise to a half hour after sunset. The trail is immensely popular, but due to its width and length it never feels overcrowded (although the parking lot may look quite full).

Bear Creek Lake Park
Owl – Fitness Trail Loop

Length: 3.1 / 3.7 mi roundtrip **Steepness:** ◢◢ 2 of 5 **Bumpy factor:** ●●● 3 of 5 **Trail surface:** dirt, sandy gravel **Trail width:** 3 - 6 ft **Trail condition:** a few large rocks, roots and ruts; some bumpy or sandy sections	**Location:** Lakewood **Distance from downtown:** 17 mi **Drive time:** 25 min **Access:** $7 per car
	Trailhead picnic tables: yes **Trailhead restrooms:** yes **Trailhead water:** yes **Playground:** nearby
Starting elevation: 5,650 ft **Elevation gain:** 100 / 150 ft	**Stroller type:** off-road tires recommended

This scenic route follows the waters of Bear Creek on its way into Bear Creek Reservoir. You run through a combination of shady creekside trails and open, exposed flatlands. An optional out-and-back spur in the middle of the route takes you to the shores of the reservoir. The route can be run or hiked with regular jogging strollers (without off-road tires), but you will need to stop and navigate several rocky sections. There is shade in the first portion of the route (Owl Trail), but none along the Fitness Loop. Bear Creek Lake Park also features a swim beach, picnic shelters, and a nice playground along the shores of Big Soda Lake.

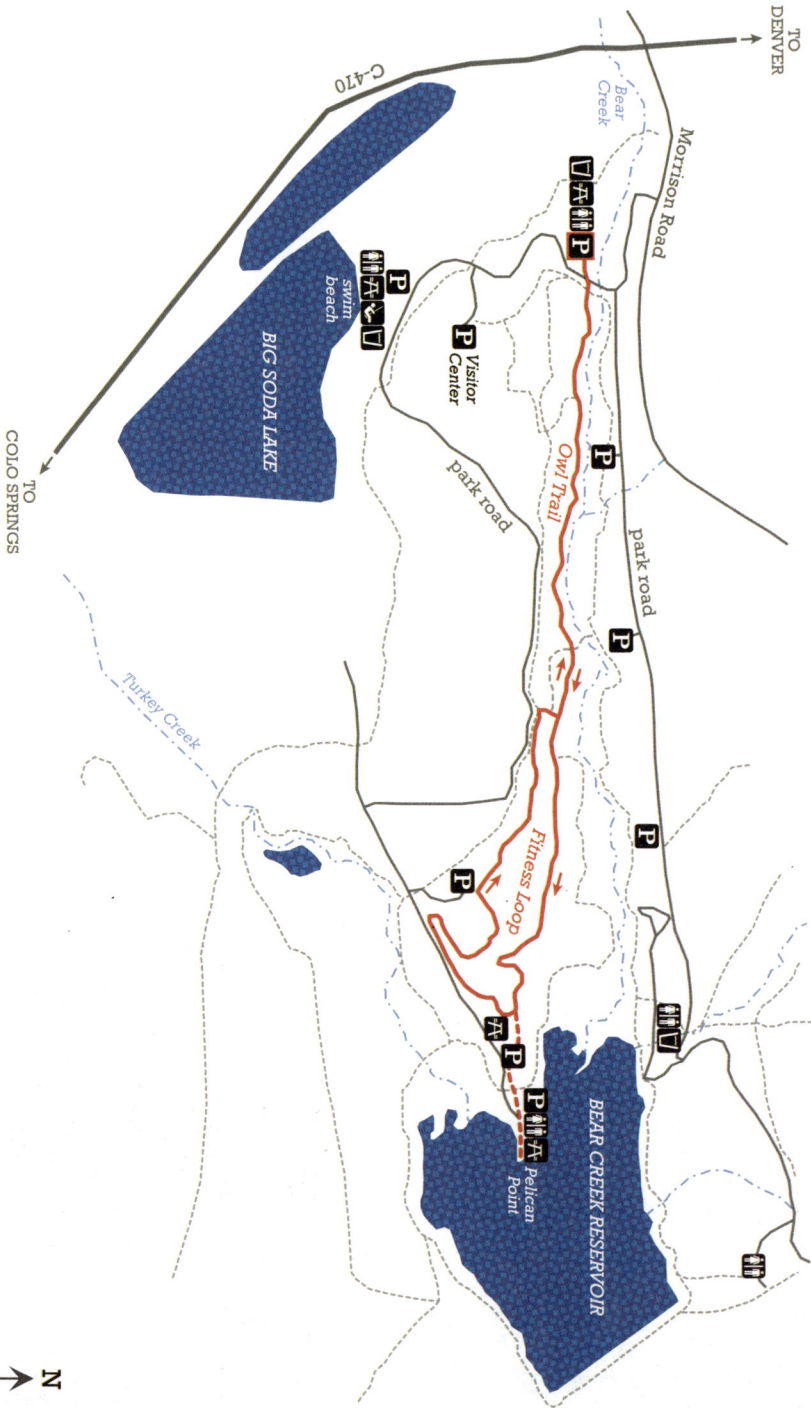

N

¼ mile

TO DENVER

TO COLO SPRINGS

C-470

BIG SODA LAKE

swim beach

Visitor Center

park road

Bear Creek

Morrison Road

park road

Owl Trail

Turkey Creek

Fitness Loop

Pelican Point

BEAR CREEK RESERVOIR

Directions

Drive west on 6th Ave and take the exit ramp to I-70 West. Keep right and merge onto C-470 East toward Colorado Springs. Head south on C-470 and exit at Morrison Road. Make a left onto Morrison Road and stay in the right lane. After 0.2 miles, turn right and follow the signs to Bear Creek Lake Park (*15600 West Morrison Rd*). Pay the entrance fee at the station and proceed on the park road. At the first intersection, turn right and cross Bear Creek. After 400 ft, enter the Skunk Hollow Picnic Area on your right and park there.

Trail Description

From the Skunk Hollow parking lot, find a wide dirt trail heading east across the park road. Join the Owl Trail as it follows the banks of Bear Creek. Here you will encounter a wooden stile as you enter the trail, just wide enough for most double strollers. The Owl Trail leads through riparian habitat and cottonwood trees for 0.7 miles, without any significant elevation changes. Stay on the path and enter the Fitness Loop, a grassland trail with 20 workout stops and fitness stations along the way. One short, steep hill requires some effort, but the remainder of the loop has only minor ups and down. The optional out-and-back spur to the shores of the reservoir adds 0.6 mi to your route: as you near the Pelican Point parking lot, leave the Fitness Trail, traverse the dirt parking lot, and find a trail near the Park Rules sign. It will take you to the tip of Pelican Point. For your return trip, rejoin the Fitness Trail loop and follow along in a clockwise direction. Just before the trail turns into a narrow singletrack, make a sharp right turn. A brief but steep downhill section completes the loop and

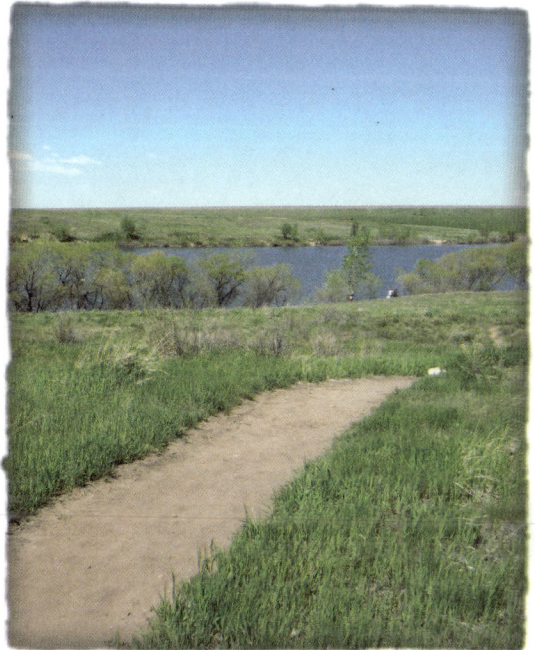

brings you back to the Owl Trail.

History & Info

This 2,600 acre park was opened in the early 1980s. During the town of Cowen's existence, coal and clay were mined here and used to manufacture bricks. Completed in 1982, Bear Creek Dam was the last of three dams built by the U.S. Army Corps of Engineers to protect the Denver region from floodwaters. Bear Creek Reservoir has an average depth of 48 feet.

Special considerations

A valid park pass is required for all vehicles. No swimming or camping is permitted except in designated areas (there is a nice swim beach at Big Soda Lake). Keep pets on a leash at all times; they are prohibited at the swim beach and in the water. The park also features a variety of paved trails which are popular with cyclists.

South Valley Park
Coyote Song / Swallow Trail

Length: 2.2 / 2.8 mi roundtrip	**Location:** Littleton
Steepness: ▲▲▲ 3 of 5	**Distance from downtown:** 24 mi
Bumpy factor: ✿✿✿ 3 of 5	**Drive time:** 30 min
Trail surface: dirt & gravel trail	**Access:** free
Trail width: 3 - 6 ft	
Trail condition: some bumps, rocks, loose sand	**Trailhead picnic tables:** yes
	Trailhead restrooms: yes
	Trailhead water: yes
	Playground: no
Starting elevation: 5,980 ft	**Stroller type:** off-road tires recommended
Elevation gain: 250 / 290 ft	

You will find nearly 1,000 acres of meadows and rocks at South Valley Park, located just west of Ken Caryl. It features the same geological sandstone formations as in Roxborough State Park (route L6), although at a smaller scale. The loop described here first winds through the meadows with lots of ups and downs, followed by a gradual uphill return. Views of the foothills and red monoliths abound. Near the parking lot, picnic tables and shelters overlooking the scenic valley are available, so plan on bringing a picnic. Avoid hot summer days here. There is a nice, shady neighborhood playground about one mile from the trailhead.

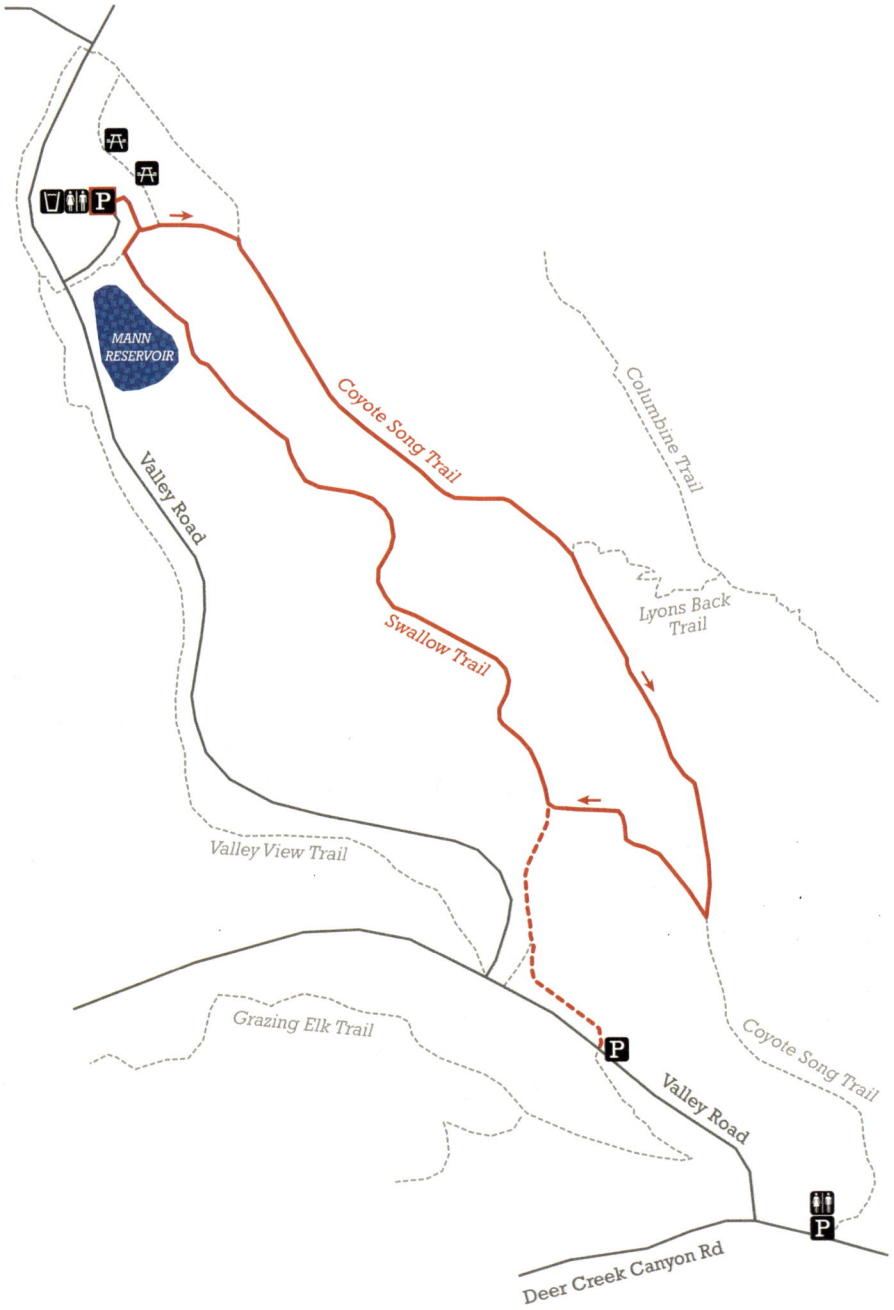

MANN RESERVOIR

Valley Road

Coyote Song Trail

Columbine Trail

Lyons Back Trail

Swallow Trail

Valley View Trail

Grazing Elk Trail

Coyote Song Trail

Valley Road

Deer Creek Canyon Rd

N

¼ mile

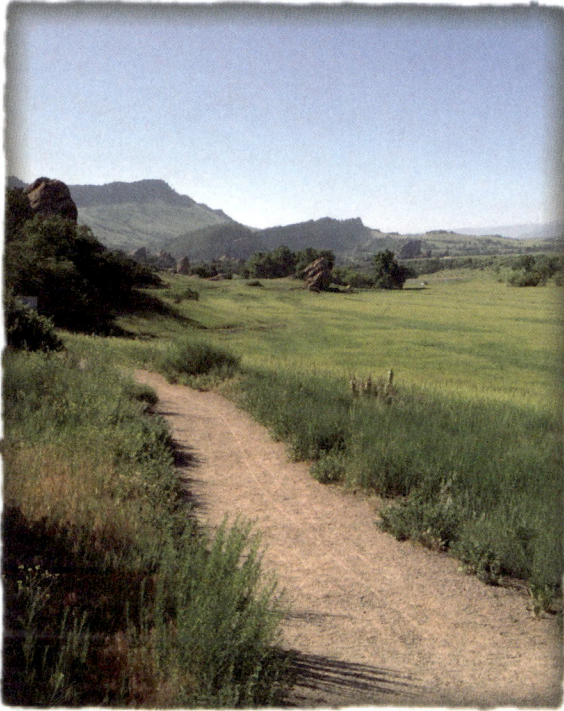

Directions

Drive west on 6th Ave and take the exit ramp to I-70 West. Keep right and merge onto C-470 East toward Colorado Springs. Head south on C-470, exit at Ken Caryl Ave and turn right. After half a mile, turn left onto Valley Road. Proceed uphill for a mile. Soon after the road dips downhill, turn left into the South Valley Park parking area.

Trail Description

The route starts with a short uphill section, bringing you to the Coyote Song Trail. Turn right and descend through the meadow. Take in the views of red sandstone spires, foothills, and the valley. After about 1 mile and several considerable hills, look for a trail intersection on your right. Make a sharp right turn and descend for 0.2 miles to reach the Swallow Trail. The optional out-and-back extension will take you through the lower meadow and to an (unofficial) parking area on Valley Road. Enjoy the (much gentler) uphill return trip on the Swallow Trail, right next to rocky cliffs and outcroppings.

History & Info

South Valley Park offers a vibrant display of the geologic processes of fault, uplift, and erosion. Several distinct formations are present in the park (and there are signs along the trails pointing out each one). Notable archeological finds in the park have established that Paleo-Indians and Indians lived in this area for over 10,000 years. More recently, the area was used for cattle breeding and raising turkeys. Jefferson County Open Space purchased the land for South Valley Park in 1997 from Lockheed-Martin. The Swallow Trail is named for the countless cliff swallows nesting in the tall rocks above the meadows. For the nearest playground, visit the neighborhood park at *24 Mountain Oak*; it has lots of shade trees and picnic tables.

Special considerations

Please do not climb on the delicate sandstone formations for your own safety and to protect these highly erosive surfaces. Park hours are 1 hour before sunrise to 1 hour after sunset. Dogs must be on a leash.

Length: 2.6 mi roundtrip **Steepness:** ▲▲▲▲ 4 of 5 **Bumpy factor:** ●● 2 of 5 **Trail surface:** dirt & gravel road; paved path **Trail width:** 5 - 10 ft **Trail condition:** smooth with some bumps and ruts	**Location:** Littleton **Distance from downtown:** 28 mi **Drive time:** 40 min **Access:** $7 per car
	Trailhead picnic tables: yes **Trailhead restrooms:** yes **Trailhead water:** yes **Playground:** no
Starting elevation: 6,190 ft **Elevation gain:** 300 ft	**Stroller type:** all types, but off-road tires will do better

Roxborough State Park sits in the lower foothills south of Denver. The park is well known for its spectacular red sandstone formations, and you will see plenty of them on this route. Ponderosa pines, Douglas firs, and prairie lands fill the scenery. Black bears, mountain lions, bobcats, golden eagles, and rattlesnakes all live here. The featured trail is short but contains a lot of uphill sections; consider making this a stroller hike rather than a run. On hot days, the tall rocks and vegetation provide some shade, but only in the early morning or in the evening hours. You may want to include educational stops at the Visitor's Center and the Fountain Valley Overlook. The nearest playground is at Roxborough Community Park, about 1.5 miles from the state park entrance.

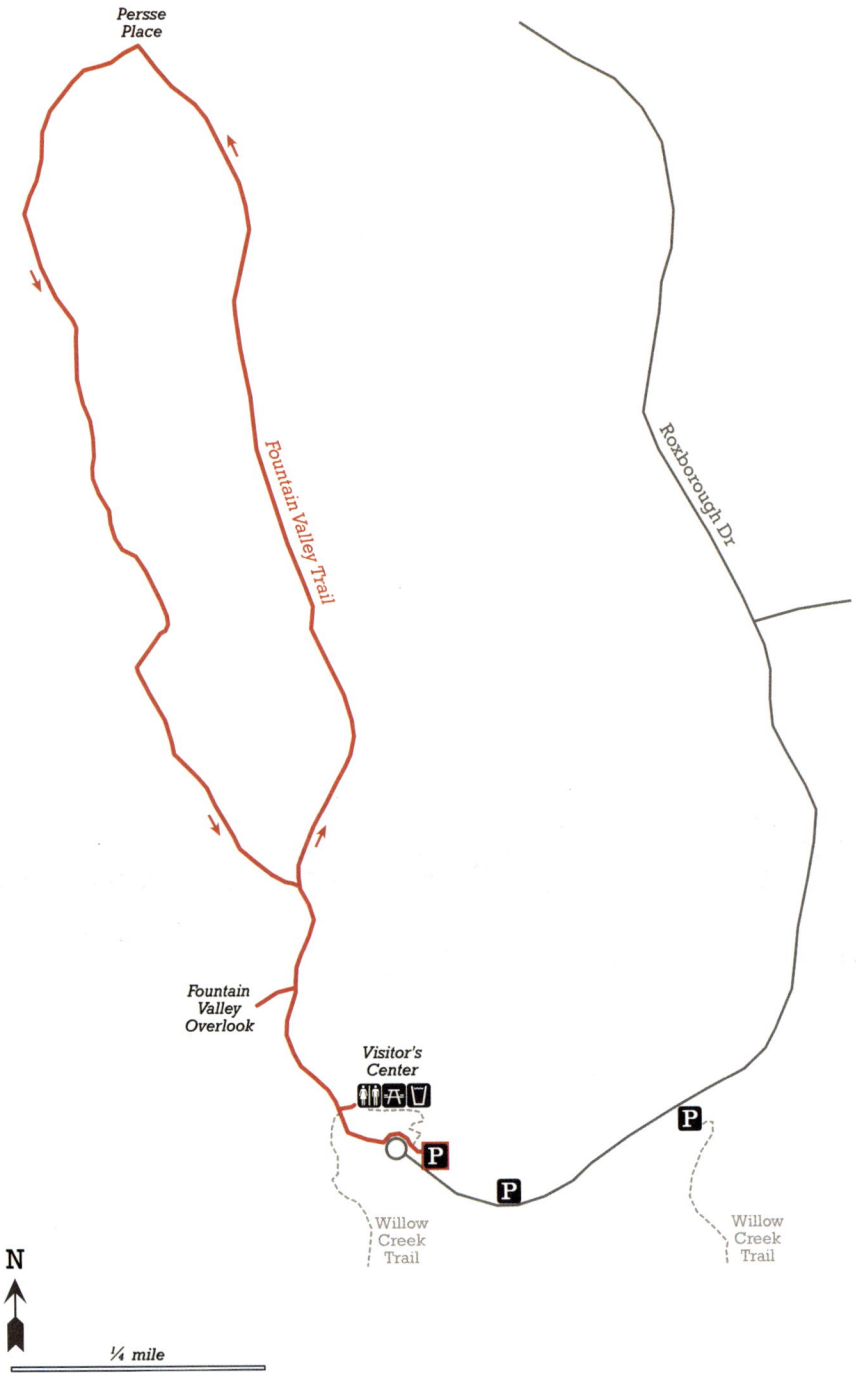

Persse Place

Fountain Valley Trail

Roxborough Dr

Fountain Valley Overlook

Visitor's Center

P

P

P

P

Willow Creek Trail

Willow Creek Trail

N

¼ mile

Directions

Drive south on I-25 and take exit 207B. Drive south on Santa Fe Drive and turn right onto C-470 West. Exit at Wadsworth Blvd and go south. Turn left onto Waterton Rd, then turn right onto Rampart Range Rd. Turn left onto Roxborough Dr and follow the signs for the state park. Park your car near the road's end.

Trail Description

From the upper parking lot, follow the sidewalk around the turnaround circle and up a paved road to the state park Visitor's Center (interpretive trail brochures for the Fountain Valley Trail are available for sale there). Join the wide, unpaved Fountain Valley Trail. After a brief climb and descent, stay right at the junction and follow the loop in a counterclockwise direction (this leaves the slightly gentler grade and shadier portion for your uphill

return). About halfway around the loop you come across Persse Place, a restored historic building worth a visit. Enjoy the stately red rock formations on the remainder of the loop. Be sure to include a short side trip to Fountain Valley Overlook before you descend to the Visitor's Center; you will be treated to amazing 360 degree views of the park.

History & Info

In the 1870s, settlers arrived in this area after the last Arapaho and Cheyenne had left. One homesteader, Henry S. Persse, used Roxborough as a summer home and planned to build a resort in the area. The state purchased the first plot of land in 1975 and Roxborough State Park was opened in 1987. The Fountain Valley Trail is named after the Fountain Formation of red sandstone in the park (this is the same type of formation you can see at Red Rocks Park and Garden of the Gods). The steep angle of these "flatiron" rocks is the result of the uplift process that created the Rockies. Their red color derives from iron-rich minerals. Nearby Roxborough Community Park has a playground, skatepark, tennis courts, and a baseball field; it is located at *7673 N Rampart Range Rd* in Littleton.

Special considerations

No pets are permitted in the state park. Trails are open 7:00 AM to 9:00 PM in the summer and 8:00 AM to 5:00 PM in the winter. No rock climbing is allowed.

L7 City of Golden - Tony Grampsas Trail

Length: 2.6 mi. **Steepness**: 2-3 of 5. **Bumpy factor**: 2 of 5. **Trail surface**: dirt & gravel path. **Trail width**: 4-6 ft. **Trail condition**: smooth with some bumps and loose gravel. **Starting elevation**: 5,630 ft. **Elevation gain**: 120 ft. **Location**: Golden. **Distance from downtown**: 14 mi. **Drive time:** 20 min. **Access**: free. **Trailhead picnic tables**: nearby. **Trailhead restrooms**: nearby. **Trailhead water**: nearby. **Playground**: nearby. **Stroller type**: all types.

Tony Grampsas Trail is a 1.3 mile trail in Golden following along the Church Ditch irrigation canal. Park in the small lot near *4789 Salvia Street* in Golden; find the unmarked trailhead across from the sign saying "Jeff Co Open Space funds used at this site". The first mile is shaded by cottonwoods and other vegetation, making this a cool trail on hot days, especially in the morning hours. When the somewhat leaky Church Ditch carries water, expect puddles on the trail. Turn around when you reach Quaker Lane. The Tony Grampsas Sports Complex near the trailhead has a playground, picnic tables, and restrooms.

L8 Jeff Co Open Space - Lookout Mountain Nature Preserve

Length: 1.5 mi. **Steepness**: 3 of 5. **Bumpy factor**: 3 of 5. **Trail surface**: gravel trail, forest floor, meadow. **Trail width**: 2-4 ft. **Trail condition**: smooth with many roots, rocks, bumps. **Starting elevation**: 7,550 ft. **Elevation gain**: 200 ft. **Location**: Golden. **Distance from downtown**: 19 mi. **Drive time:** 30 min. **Access**: free. **Trailhead picnic tables**: yes. **Trailhead restrooms**: yes. **Trailhead water**: yes. **Playground**: no. **Stroller type**: double strollers not encouraged due to trail width.

High above Golden sits the peaceful Lookout Mountain Nature Center & Preserve. For this short route, start at the Nature Center; string together the Forest Loop Trail and the Meadow Loop Trail into a figure-8 loop. Return via the Boettcher Mansion. You will encounter pine forests and lush grassy open space. This scenic route is better hiked than run. The address is *910 Colorow Rd* in Golden.

Lair o' the Bear Park
Bear Creek Trail

Length: 4.1 mi roundtrip **Steepness:** ◢◢ 2 of 5 **Bumpy factor:** ✦✦✦✦ 4 of 5 **Trail surface:** dirt road, gravel trail **Trail width:** 2 - 5 ft **Trail condition:** some rocky segments, ruts, roots, creek crossings	**Location:** Morrison **Distance from downtown:** 21 mi **Drive time:** 35 min **Access:** free
	Trailhead picnic tables: yes **Trailhead restrooms:** yes **Trailhead water:** no **Playground:** no
Starting elevation: 6,500 ft **Elevation gain:** 250 ft	**Stroller type:** off-road tires recommended; no double strollers

With the picturesque babbling stream at your side, this route climbs gently through Bear Creek Canyon upstream of the town of Morrison. The cool banks of Bear Creek provide ample shade. Every few minutes you encounter rocks and ruts, but in between the trail is smooth and wide. Double strollers are not recommended due to several narrow trail sections. Many hikers, mountain bikers, and fly fishermen frequent this trail on weekends, so it is best to visit during the week.

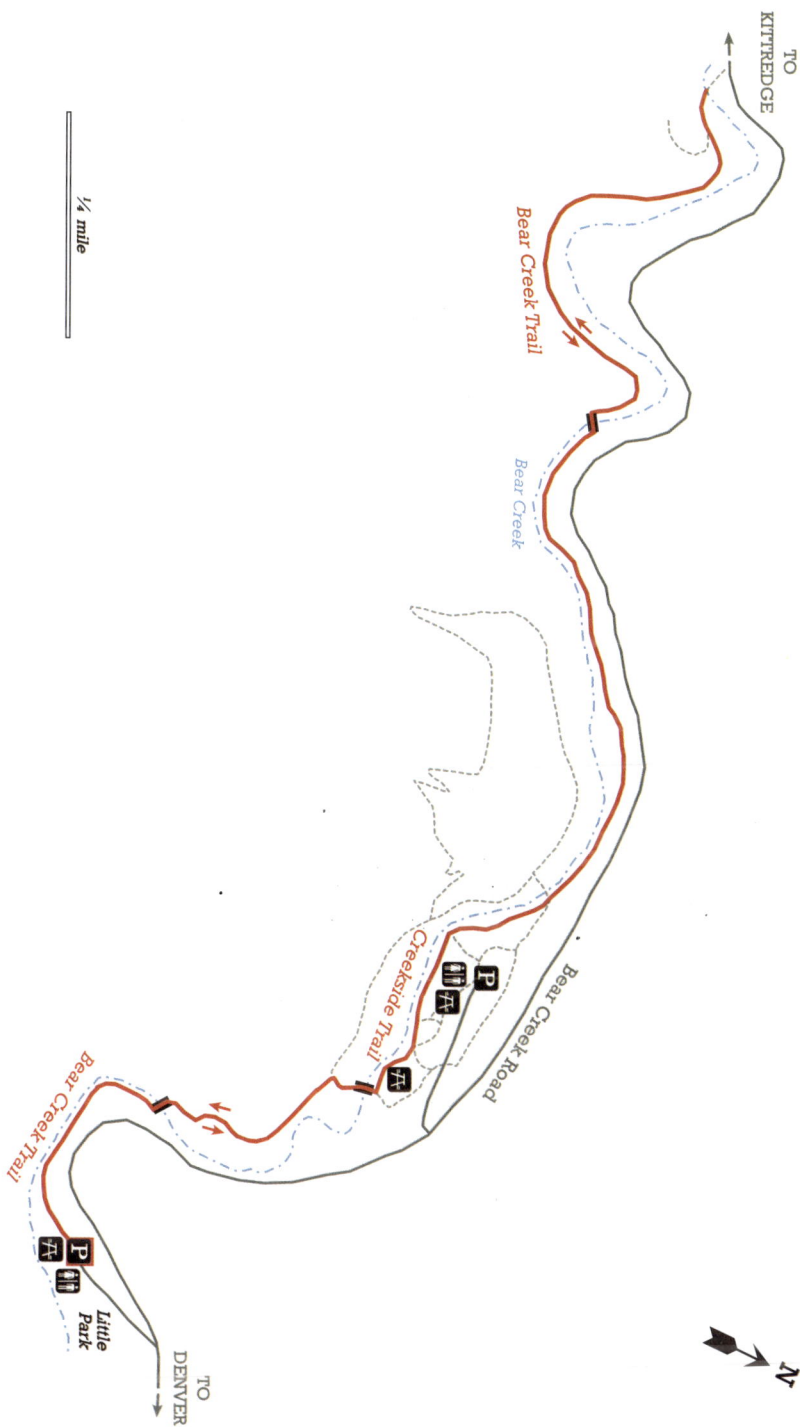

TO KITTREDGE

Bear Creek Trail

Bear Creek

Creekside Trail

Bear Creek Road

Bear Creek Trail

Little Park

TO DENVER

¼ mile

N

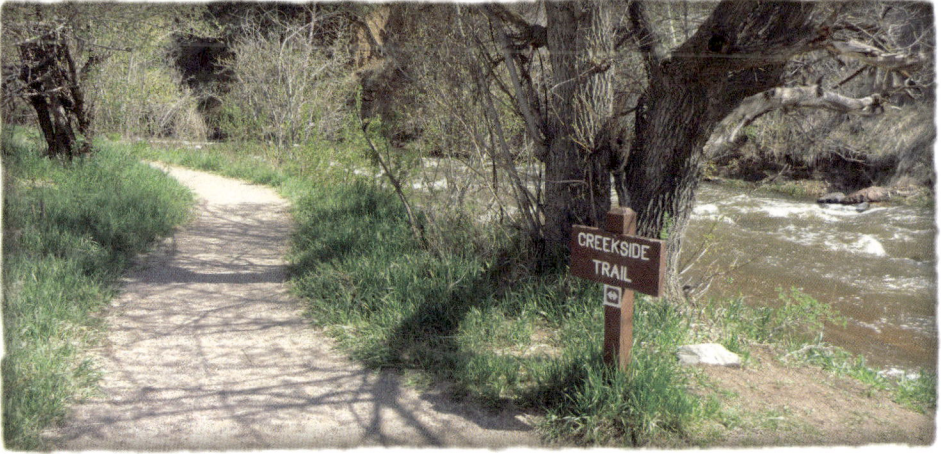

Directions

Drive west on 6th Ave and take the exit ramp to I-70 West. Keep right and merge onto C-470 East toward Colorado Springs. Head south on C-470 and exit at Morrison Road (Highway 74). Make a right onto Morrison Road and follow it through the town of Morrison for 4.5 miles. Just past the town of Idledale, make a left turn onto a downhill dirt access road (this turnoff is easily missed). There is a parking lot at Little Park, along with restrooms and picnic tables.

Trail Description

The route begins at Little Park and follows an old dirt road upriver. Cross the first of 3 bridges on this route and continue on the other side of the creek. Here the trail is at its narrowest, with some rocks and ruts. At 0.6 miles make a right turn at the Bruin Bluff Trail junction and cross the creek again. Immediately turn left and follow the stream closely, passing through picnic areas and fishing decks (you are now on the Creekside Trail). This area contains the main parking lot and is often the busiest in the park. Ignore the many side trails; when in doubt, follow the creek. Rejoin the Bear Creek Trail and continue to meander alongside the creek. This section has two crossings through intermittent streams (usually just shallow trickles of water, except in the spring). Here several narrow, rocky segments may require walking your stroller. You will then run along forested creek banks and pass a private home which is built like a castle (complete with a moat) on your right. Cross the final bridge and proceed to the turnaround point: a gate before a concrete bridge leading to Bear Creek Road. The Bear Creek Trail continues on to Corwina Park, but it is much steeper and narrower past this point.

History & Info

In the second half of the 19th century, the town of Morrison was an important mining supply town. Later, the area was used for farming. In the early 1900s, Swedish settlers grew many varieties of produce here; they delivered it to Denver and Evergreen by truck. Three log dams were constructed on Bear Creek to irrigate the fields and orchards. A few apple and cherry trees can still be found today in Lair o' the Bear Park. In the 1930s, farmland was converted to grazing land. The park was purchased by Jefferson County Open Space in 1987.

Special considerations

Dogs must be on a leash. Park hours are 1 hour before sunrise to 1 hour after sunset. It is your responsibility to know and obey Open Space rules and regulations.

Mount Falcon Park
Castle Trail (west)

Length: 2.7 mi roundtrip **Steepness:** ▲▲▲▲▲ 5 of 5 **Bumpy factor:** ●●● 3 of 5 **Trail surface:** dirt & gravel road **Trail width:** 6 - 12 ft **Trail condition:** rocks, roots, and bumps	**Location:** Morrison **Distance from downtown:** 27 mi **Drive time:** 35 min **Access:** free
	Trailhead picnic tables: yes **Trailhead restrooms:** yes **Trailhead water:** no **Playground:** no
Starting elevation: 7,770 ft **Elevation gain:** 400 ft	**Stroller type:** off-road tires recommended

Mount Falcon Park sits high up in the Front Range foothills, yet its close proximity to Denver makes it a popular getaway. The park has two entrances; this trail starts at the higher west side entrance. The route is short but sweet and makes a beautiful hike or a challenging run with scenic views and lots of ups and downs. The trail is wide but bumpy in places and it showcases the Front Range foothills terrain at its best: stands of pines trees, wildflower meadows, boulders, and rock outcroppings. The trail also visits the historic ruins of John Walker's home. There are a lot of picnic tables and shelters near the parking area; the most scenic picnic spots are just below the parking lot, overlooking the Parmalee Gulch valley. Avoid summer weekends - it can get crowded up here. There is a nice playground a few minutes from the trailhead on Parmalee Gulch Road.

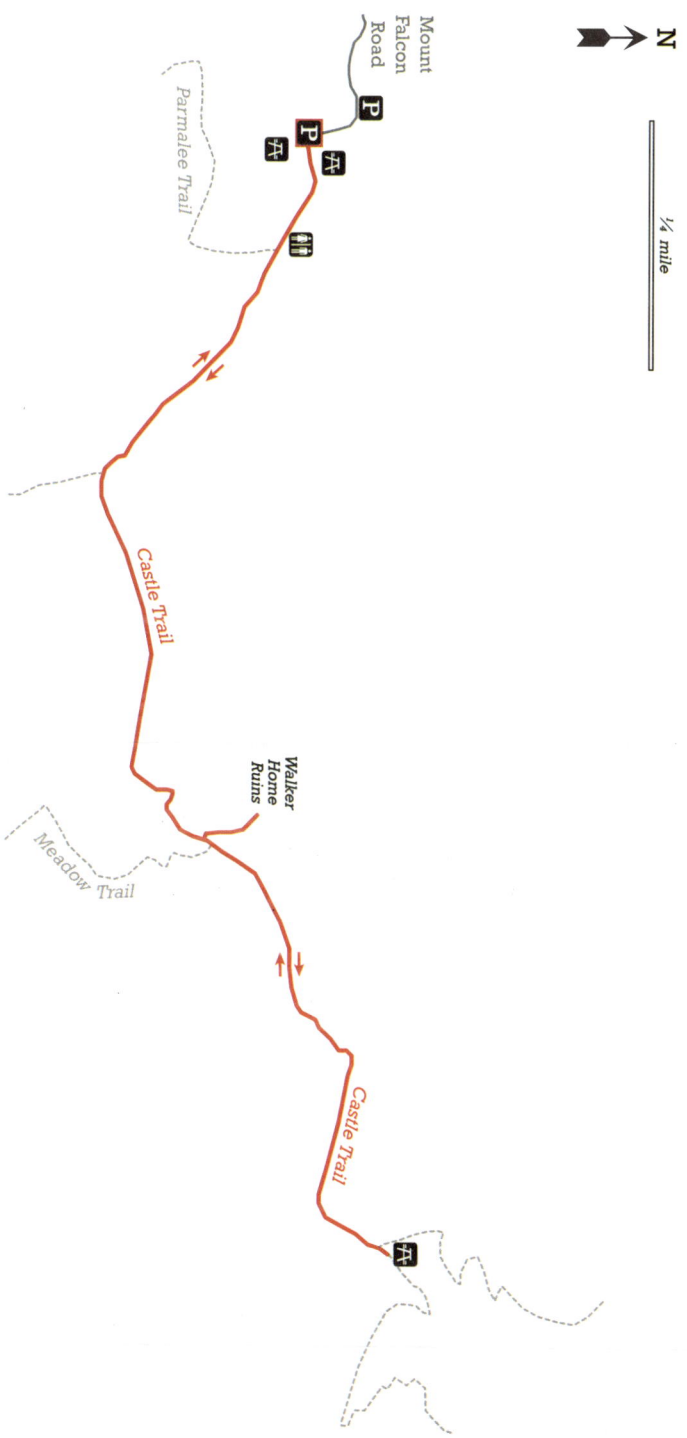

N

¼ mile

Mount
Falcon
Road

P

P

Parmalee Trail

Castle Trail

Walker
Home
Ruins

Meadow Trail

Castle Trail

111

Directions

Drive west on 6th Ave. Take the exit to I-70, keep right and merge onto C-470 East toward Colorado Springs. Head south on C-470 and exit at Hwy 285 South toward Fairplay. Proceed on Hwy 285 for 4.5 miles and exit at Parmalee Gulch Rd. Turn right and continue uphill on Parmalee Gulch Rd for 2.7 miles, turn right onto Picutis Rd, then make an immediate left turn onto Comanche Rd. After 0.1 miles, turn right onto Ohkay Rd, then turn right again onto Picutis Rd. Stay on the paved road for about 1.5 miles until it dead-ends at Mount Falcon Park (*21000 Mt Falcon Rd*). There is a fantastic playground at Arrowhead Community Park, about 0.3 miles from the Picutis Rd turnoff (*4480 Parmalee Gulch Rd*). That park also features a volleyball court, a restroom, and picnic shelters.

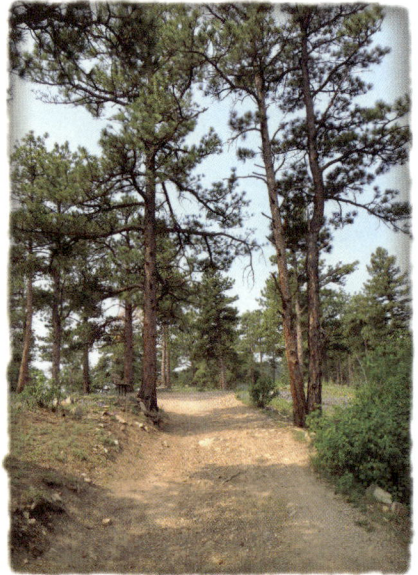

Trail Description

The Castle Trail is easy to follow on its wide up and down course through meadows and trees. There is some shade under the pine trees, but not continuously. When you reach the sign for Walker Home Ruins, continue straight on the Castle Trail, leaving

the visit to the ruins as a break during your return leg. Descend for another 0.5 miles. Turn around when you reach the picnic shelter at the Walkers Dream intersection. Beyond this point, the Castle Trail is considerably steeper and narrower. On your way back, take the short detour to the Walker Home Ruins before continuing your uphill trip back to the parking area.

History & Info

John Brisben Walker, a millionaire from West Virginia, purchased this area as a homestead in the early 1900s. The Castle Trail is named after the grand home he

constructed in 1909 for his family using native rock (it burned down in 1918). Before encountering financial problems, he made plans to build a "summer White House" for U.S. presidents, but the project was never completed. He was a strong proponent of building a Denver mountain park system; Mount Falcon was made a public park in 1974 by the Colorado Open Lands Foundation and Jefferson County Open Space.

Special considerations

Dogs must be on a leash. Park hours are 1 hour before sunrise to 1 hour after sunset.

Elk Meadow Park
Painters Pause Trail

Length: 3.3 / 4.0 mi roundtrip
Steepness: ▲▲▲▲▲ 5 of 5
Bumpy factor: ✹✹✹✹ 4 of 5
Trail surface: gravel & dirt path, forest floor
Trail width: 2 - 6 ft
Trail condition: sections with rocks, ruts, roots, or loose gravel

Location: Evergreen
Distance from downtown: 23 mi
Drive time: 30 min
Access: free

Trailhead picnic tables: nearby
Trailhead restrooms: yes
Trailhead water: no
Playground: nearby

Starting elevation: 7,750 ft
Elevation gain: 440 / 530 ft

Stroller type: off-road tires recommended; duallies not encouraged

If you have heard that Elk Meadow Park is just for mountain bikers and hard-core hikers, think again. This lovely route skirts the steeper singletrack trails for a scenic run through the meadows that give the park its name. However, since the meadows are situated on an incline, there are a lot of ups and downs. The vegetation varies from open grasslands with sparse trees to pine forest. As there is little shade, it can get quite hot in the summer. The meadows are full of wildflowers by July and you may see deer or elk at the edge of the forest. The trail runs close to Evergreen Parkway for part of the way, but other sections feel quite remote. There is a playground at Buchanan Fields (near the trailhead) and a larger one less than 2.5 miles away at Stagecoach Park.

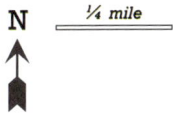

N ¼ mile

TO
DENVER

Squaw Pass Road

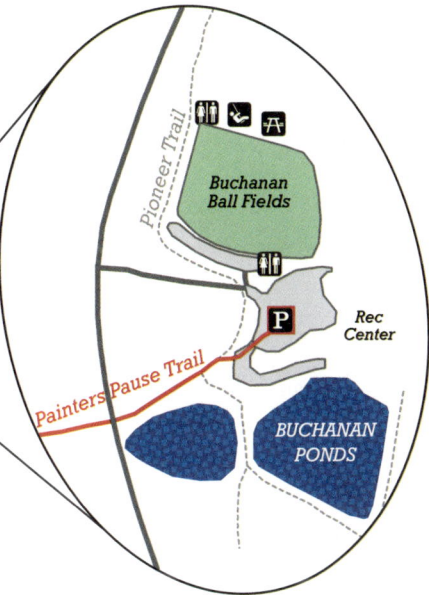

Pioneer Trail

Buchanan
Ball Fields

Rec
Center

P

Painters Pause Trail

BUCHANAN
PONDS

Painters
Pause
Trail

Evergreen Parkway

Meadow
View
Trail

Founders Trail

Bergen Creek

Sleepy S Trail

P

TO
EVERGREEN

Directions

Drive west on 6th Ave and to I-70 West. Exit I-70 at Evergreen Parkway. Drive past the town of Bergen Park. Turn left at the intersection with Squaw Pass Road and follow the short road downhill. Park at the Buchanan Ball Fields to your left or at the Buchanan Park Rec Center to your right. The trailhead is located near one of the ponds, right by the Evergreen Parkway underpass (*32299 Ellingwood Trail*). If you enjoy Italian food, try the Tuscany Tavern right by the trailhead; it is our family's favorite local Italian restaurant and features outdoor seating for the kids.

Trail Description

Find the Painters Pause Trail and pass under Evergreen Parkway. Follow the trail for 0.7 miles as it traverses steeply up and down through the meadow hills. Here the trail is a wide gravel path. Turn right at the junction with Meadow View Trail and continue 0.5 miles on a gentle climb to the forest edge. Ruts and rocks can be found on this mostly double track segment. Turn left onto Founders Trail and enjoy the view of the entire meadow. This downhill section has some narrow segments with rocks and roots. At the junction with Painters Pause Trail, either turn left and return to the trailhead, or turn right and proceed downhill on the gradually narrowing Painters Pause Trail. Turn back when you reach the intersection with the Sleepy-S

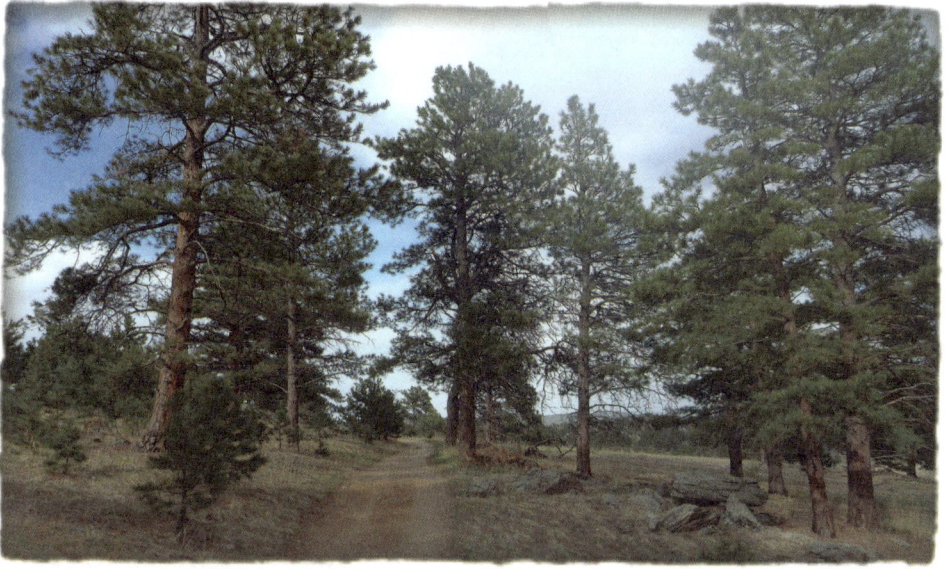

Trail. This optional out-and-back segment adds about 0.7 miles and 90 feet of elevation to your route.

History & Info

Starting in the 1860s, the U.S. Government offered homesteaders 160-acre tracts of land in the Evergreen Township. By the 1940s, Darst Buchanan had bought thousands of acres to maintain his large herd of cattle. In 1949, Cole Means purchased some of Buchanan's land as a summer pasture for his own herds. In 1975, Jefferson County Open Space began acquiring this property. A picturesque barn in the meadow remains as evidence of the park's ranching history.

Special considerations

Park hours are 1 hour before sunrise to 1 hour after sunset. Dogs must be leashed. Keep in mind that this route is frequently used by mountain bikers and hikers, so expect to share the trail. A large playground is located at Stagecoach Park off Evergreen Parkway (*3216 El Pinal Drive*).

F4 Pine Valley Ranch Park - Narrow Gauge Trail

Length: 2.0 mi. **Steepness**: 2 of 5. **Bumpy factor**: 3 of 5. **Trail surface**: dirt road, forest floor. **Trail width**: 5-8 ft. **Trail condition**: smooth with ruts and rocks. **Starting elevation**: 6,850 ft. **Elevation gain**: 100 ft. **Location**: Pine. **Distance from downtown**: 46 mi. **Drive time**: 55 min. **Access**: free. **Trailhead picnic tables**: yes. **Trailhead restrooms**: yes. **Trailhead water**: yes. **Playground**: no. **Stroller type**: double strollers not recommended.

This peaceful trail follows an old railroad bed next to the South Platte River near the community of Pine. It is a mostly flat multi-use trail that connects to other trails in the park. Some sections of the trail resemble a double track road, so wide strollers are not recommended. Begin at the main parking lot at the end of Crystal Lake Rd and turn right at the bridge. Follow the out-and-back Narrow Gauge Trail upriver, passing by two more bridges. A good point to turn around is at the Park Boundary marker by a small creek crossing. For a longer route, continue on the Narrow Gauge Trail downriver past the parking lot; it is narrower and slightly steeper here, but also more scenic. Let the kids explore the wide Pine Lake Loop trail around Baehr Reservoir (Pine Lake) with its viewing areas and benches. The trailhead is located at *30500 Crystal Lake Rd* in Pine.

F5 Alderfer/Three Sisters Park - Meadow / Wild Iris Loop

Length: 2.0 mi. **Steepness**: 3 of 5. **Bumpy factor**: 4 of 5. **Trail surface**: gravel, forest floor, meadow. **Trail width**: 2-4 ft. **Trail condition**: some roots; rocky/sandy sections; a few water bars. **Starting elevation**: 7,710 ft. **Elevation gain**: 150 ft. **Location**: Evergreen. **Distance from downtown**: 31 mi. **Drive time**: 45 min. **Access**: free. **Trailhead picnic tables**: yes. **Trailhead restrooms**: yes. **Trailhead water**: no. **Playground**: no. **Stroller type**: double strollers not encouraged due to trail width.

Three Sisters Park is known for its technical mountain bike trails, but this scenic meadow two-loop route is suitable for strollers. Most of the trail is smooth, but a few narrow sections and roots and rocks will slow you down considerably (especially on the second loop). From the west parking lot first run or hike along the counterclockwise loop formed by the Meadow Trail, Silver Fox Trail, Homestead Trail, and Bluebird Trail. For an additional half mile, at the junction with the Homestead Trail, continue on the Silver Fox Trail to where it meets the Ponderosa Trail (it becomes too steep and rocky beyond that), then turn back and complete the loop back to the parking lot. For the second loop, proceed along the Wild Iris Loop in a counterclockwise direction. For fewer mountain bike encounters, visit the park during the week. The trailhead is located at *5182 S Lemasters Rd* in Evergreen.

F6 Flying J Ranch Park - Shadow Pine Loop

Length: 2.8 mi. **Steepness**: 3 of 5. **Bumpy factor**: 5 of 5. **Trail surface**: dirt trail, forest floor. **Trail width**: 3-5 ft. **Trail condition**: roots, large rocks, one creek crossing. **Starting elevation**: 8,060 ft. **Elevation gain**: 270 ft. **Location**: Conifer. **Distance from downtown**: 33 mi. **Drive time:** 40 min. **Access**: free. **Trailhead picnic tables**: yes. **Trailhead restrooms**: yes. **Trailhead water**: no. **Playground**: no. **Stroller type**: double strollers not recommended; off-road tires required.

This trail near Conifer is a challenging route in a wonderful mountain setting. It is not overly steep, but the high altitude and a few sections with large rocks add to its difficulty. Nearly the entire trail is shaded by trees (there are a few open meadows). Run or walk the Shadow Pine Loop in a clockwise direction, taking care to stay on the main trail at all intersections. The most difficult segments are in the final

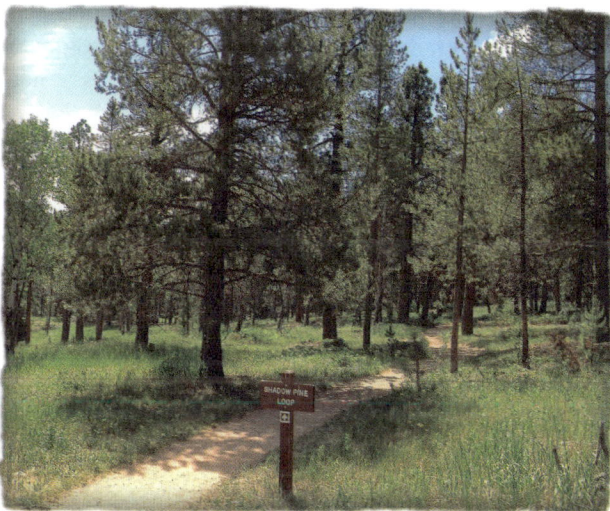

half mile, including a rocky creek crossing that may require you to walk or carry your stroller across the wet boulders. The parking area features several very scenic picnic sites, so bring some yummy food and enjoy the forest! The park entrance is located at *9616 CO-73* in Conifer.

F7 Evergreen - Evergreen Lake Trail

Length: 2.5 mi. **Steepness**: 3-4 of 5. **Bumpy factor**: 2 of 5. **Trail surface**: gravel and dirt path; boardwalks. **Trail width**: 4-6 ft. **Trail condition**: mostly smooth, some rocks. **Starting elevation**: 7,080 ft. **Elevation gain**: 90 ft. **Location**: Evergreen. **Distance from downtown**: 28 mi. **Drive time**: 40 min. **Access**: free. **Trailhead picnic tables**: yes. **Trailhead restrooms**: yes. **Trailhead water**: yes. **Playground**: no. **Stroller type**: double strollers not encouraged due to steepness.

A beautiful lake in a scenic setting, Evergreen Lake features a perimeter trail that's partially on wooden boardwalks, partially along Bear Creek Road, and partially in the forest. The trail is immensely popular; try to avoid it on weekends. It forms a 1.3 mile loop, but the many steep steps at the dam make stroller access impossible. Instead, from the Evergreen Lake House parking lot, first proceed along the north shore trail and turn back at the dam; then, complete the south shore trail and return, for a 2.5 mile total roundtrip. Most of the trail is rather flat but several steep ascents (especially on the south side) will remind you that you are at 7,000 feet elevation. This route is better as a stroller hike than a run. The trailhead is located near *29500 Upper Bear Creek Rd* in Evergreen.